FLESH AND BLOOD

FLESH AND BLOOD

A Dogmatic Sketch Concerning the Fallen Nature View of Christ's Human Nature

Daniel J. Cameron

Foreword by Myk Habets

WIPF & STOCK · Eugene, Oregon

FLESH AND BLOOD
A Dogmatic Sketch Concerning the Fallen Nature
View of Christ's Human Nature

Wipf & Stock
An Imprint of Wipf and Stock Publishers
199 W. 8th Ave., Suite 3
Eugene, OR 97401

www.wipfandstock.com

PAPERBACK ISBN: 978-1-4982-3272-2
HARDCOVER ISBN: 978-1-4982-3274-6
EBOOK ISBN: 978-1-4982-3273-9

Manufactured in the U.S.A.   10/05/16

To my dad, "Captain" Ron Cameron (1961–2013), and to my great-grandmother, Elsie Frazier (1920–2013)

Contents

Foreword

God's Journey into the Far Country

ONE OF THE CENTRAL mysteries of the faith is the revealed fact that Christ has reconciled God and humanity not by some external transaction but by his full assumption of human flesh and his perfect life, death, and resurrection. Essential to any valid view of the atonement is the fact that we must view redemption and reconciliation as something internal to the being of Christ and not simply as an external transaction. The saving act of God in Christ was internal to the incarnate Son before it could be applied externally. Redemption, reconciliation, and salvation in all its aspects are not simply an external arrangement between God and humanity, or between Christ and the world. Rather, "if the soteriological exchange takes place within the constitution of the incarnate Person of the Mediator, then it is as eternal as Jesus Christ himself, the eternal Son,"[1] as Thomas Torrance reminds us. Throughout the life of the incarnate Son an atoning exchange is made once and for all as human nature is taken up and given a place in God and thus grounded in his eternal unchangeable reality. By human nature we refer, in the first instance, to the humanity of Jesus Christ. In the incarnate person of the Son an ontological atonement has been perfectly accomplished—God and humanity have been reconciled once and for all. It is on this basis that believers may also be saved but only in, by, and through Jesus Christ.

When salvation is construed externally to Christ, it is instrumentalized and made conditional upon factors additional to

1. Torrance, *The Trinitarian Faith*, 183–84.

those found in Jesus. In Roman Catholicism a form of sacramental penance is required to attain merit with God and so attain to grace; within forms of Protestantism other meritorious actions are required, with often faith and repentance being conceived as works rather than free responses of the individual to saving grace. Such accounts of salvation are semi-Pelagian at their foundations and recommend a form of co-redemption. In order to avoid such unorthodox accounts of the saving significance of Christ, an ontological theory of the atonement is required in which Christ is the sole mediator between humanity and God.

Thomas Torrance, whose theology is a focus of the present book, presents an ontological theory of incarnational redemption. This ontological atonement, mediation, or redemption forms the first stage of salvation proper in Torrance's theology, characterized by the sanctification of Christ's own human nature. As Torrance articulates it:

> [Christ] had come, Son of God incarnate as Son of man, in order to get to grips with the powers of darkness and defeat them, but he had been sent to do that not through the manipulation of social, political or economic power-structures, but by striking beneath them all into the ontological depths of Israel's existence where man, and Israel representing all mankind, had become estranged from God, and there within those ontological depths of human being to forge a bond of union and communion between man and God in himself which can never be undone.[2]

At the cross God meets, suffers, and triumphs over the enmity entrenched in human existence once and for all, in Jesus Christ. Ontological atonement has been achieved in the incarnate life and death of the Son of God, confirmed in the resurrection from the empty tomb, and initiated in the sending of the Spirit at Pentecost.[3]

The human life of Christ contains redemptive value in the sense that it completes the efficacy of the incarnation. For full

2. Torrance, *The Mediation of Christ*, 30.
3. Ibid., 31.

redemption and reconciliation to occur the eternal Son of God assumed our natural—fallen—human condition in order to divinize human life in its various stages. That is to say, in the words of Jules Gross, "he lived it personally."[4] This does not imply that an ontological theory of the atonement suggests in any way a mechanical salvation for men and women, the physical theory *simpliciter*. There are processes or stages to be followed by which human beings in general may be saved (or deified) including the sacraments and the Christian life. Before discussing that, however, the ontological basis for salvation must first of all be a reality in the life of the incarnate Word, Jesus Christ. The work of salvation is supremely the work of Christ (with God the Father and the Holy Spirit), to whom the initiative goes completely.

Advocates of an ontological theory of the Incarnation, such as Thomas Torrance, repeatedly advocate the axiom of Gregory of Nazianzus: "that which has not been assumed has not been healed."[5] Torrance uses this phrase in at least two senses: first, that Christ assumed a complete or total human nature, the sense that Gregory of Nazianzus appears to have made of it (an anti-Apollinarian argument); and second, that Christ has completely healed humanity in his own incarnation. This is what Torrance means by a doctrine of deification applied to the hypostatic union.[6] On the basis of Jesus' deification of *his* human nature he is now able to deify or save others who are united to himself.

The result is that Christ has totally redeemed, reconciled, cleansed, lifted, restored, and recreated human nature to what God had intended it to be in the first place.[7] The consummation of deified humanity is centred upon the summing up of all things in Christ, when he transforms us in the whole of our human nature.

---

4. Gross, *The Divinization of the Christian*, 171, applied these words to Athanasius' doctrine of Christ's *theosis*.

5. Gregory, "To Cledonius," 440. See Torrance, "Incarnation and Atonement," 12; "The Atonement the Singularity of Christ," 237–39; and *The Christian Doctrine of God*, 250.

6. Torrance, *The Trinitarian Faith*, 188–90.

7. See Torrance, *Space, Time and Resurrection*, 139.

"When we see him we shall become like him, and when we become like him we shall see him with healed vision and recreated natures."[8] The uniting of human and divine natures in the one person of the incarnate Son achieves salvation; it divinizes human nature ontologically. This has yet to be applied to other human beings but the important point is that it has been achieved in the God-man. This is what qualifies the Son to be the Mediator and Saviour of humanity.

In the incarnation the eternal Son of God assumes fallen human nature and redeems it thus restoring and fulfilling the divine *telos* for humanity of union and communion with God.[9] With Athanasius, Torrance speaks of Jesus as "the Dominical Man" and "the principle of ways" which God has provided for us. By this he means that the incarnate Christ has an archetypal significance for human beings.[10] He even suggests that: "every human being is ontologically bound to him. It is in Jesus Christ the incarnate Creator, then, that the being of all men, whether they believe or not, is creatively grounded and is unceasingly sustained."[11] The chief end and true felicity of humanity involves, according to Torrance, knowledge of oneself as a creature utterly dependent on the grace of God.

Of great importance then for any account of the atonement is the issue of Christ's humanity—specifically the question: Was

8. Ibid., 140.

9. This is a reversal of the fall which resulted in sin which Torrance defines as shattered communion in Torrance, "The Atoning Obedience of Christ," 65–66.

10. Torrance, "The Soul and Person," 115–16.

11. Torrance, "The Atonement the Singularity of Christ," 244. Torrance is not implying that all people, by right of this ontological bond, are saved. Quite the opposite! The article in question is one in which Torrance is arguing for the singularity of Christ in an otherwise pluralistic world. His point is that because Jesus Christ is the Creator Incarnate, then all creation, men and women especially, are ontologically related to him. His logic goes as follows: if Christ in his incarnation represents all humanity, then in his atonement he must represent to the same extent all humanity. Any other view is to separate atonement from incarnation and revert back to an old dualist notion: a "schizoid notion of the incarnation" (ibid., 246).

Christ's humanity of the fallen stock of Adam or was it untouched by Adam's sin? Throughout the history of popular Christian thinking the normative status of humanity has most often been ascribed to Adam and Eve in their pre-lapsarian condition rather than to the humanity of Jesus Christ in his incarnation, resulting in a general affirmation that Christ did not assume a fallen human nature. Torrance, and those convinced by his theological claims, has consistently adopted the contrary position: that the eternal Son assumed a *fallen* human nature, and he argues that this is essential in a full articulation of the gospel.

> If the incarnate Son through his birth of the Virgin Mary actually assumed our flesh of sin, the fallen, corrupt and enslaved human nature which we have all inherited from Adam, then the redeeming activity of Christ took place within the ontological depths of his humanity in such a way that far from sinning himself, he condemned sin in the flesh and sanctified what he assumed, so that incarnating and redeeming events were one and indivisible, from the very beginning of his earthly existence to its end in his death and resurrection.[12]

Torrance's argument hangs on the concept of a *vicarious* assumption of human nature in its fallenness and sin. Christ did not, according to this logic, inherit sin naturally and so, unlike all other children of Adam, he had no natural sin-nature or morally culpable stain of original sin.[13] However, through an assumption of human nature in its post-lapsarian condition, Christ could remain guilt-free while still assuming a *vicarious* and fallen human nature. Torrance is thoroughly patristic when he attributes sin to the person-*hypostasis*, not as Augustine (and the West) did, to essence or nature. This accounts for why Christ could assume the likeness of sinful flesh (nature) and yet remain sinless (person). Considered *anhypostatically,* Christ has a sin-*nature,* albeit vicariously.

---

12. Torrance, "Incarnation and Atonement," 12.

13. For a constructive account of what original sin is in this reconceived theology see Habets, "'Suffer the little children.'"

Considered *enhypostatically*, Christ is sinless for his *person* is consonant with that of the eternal Son of God.[14]

Donald Macleod claims that Torrance "went on to reintroduce to Scotland the peculiar Christology of Edward Irving," and so Macleod calls this the "Irving-Torrance theory."[15] This conclusion is far too simplistic, however. Torrance does speak of Irving as providing some useful resources showing that the Son assumed a fallen human nature and so in this, Irving and Torrance are at one. However, Torrance is at odds with how Irving sought to account for this assumed nature. For instance, Torrance wishes to avoid the two extremes that could result from a consideration of the vicarious humanity of Christ: on the one hand Ebionite, and on the other hand docetic views. Torrance believes Irving espoused an Ebionite Christology because he held that the sinlessness of Christ was due to the indwelling Holy Spirit not to his own nature. On the docetic side Torrance suggests that certain notions of the "deification" of Christ's human nature are to be ruled out; notions which would mix or confuse the human and divine natures in such a way that the human nature disappears.[16] In *Space, Time and Resurrection* Torrance further articulates how Christ remains sinless despite vicariously assuming a fallen human nature: "Although he assumed our fallen and corrupt humanity when he became flesh, in assuming it he sanctified it in himself, and all through his earthly life he overcame our sin through his righteousness, our impurity through his purity, condemning sin in our flesh by the sheer holiness of his life within it."[17]

Torrance goes on to say that this is precisely why death could not hold Christ (cf. Acts 2:24) for there was no sin in him that allowed it to subject him to corruption. Death had nothing in him, for he had already passed through its clutches by the perfection

14. Torrance, *The Doctrine of Jesus Christ*, 121–30; and "The Atonement the Singularity of Christ," 237–39.

15. Macleod, "Christology," 175. See the longer discussions in his, *Jesus is Lord*, 125–34; and *The Person of Christ*, 221–30.

16. Torrance, *The Doctrine of Jesus Christ*, 121–23.

17. Torrance, *Space, Time and Resurrection*, 53.

of his holiness. In short, "He triumphed over the grave through his sheer sinlessness."[18] He then concludes with the statement that, "The resurrection is thus the resurrection of the union forged between man and God in Jesus out of the damned and lost condition of men into which Christ entered in order to share their lot and redeem them from doom."[19] Such a focus on Christ's assumption of a fallen human nature, despite its attendant difficulties, clearly highlights the depths to which Torrance believes Christ descended in saving humanity.

Torrance's account is clear and compelling, and yet, for many, it is not convincing. Recent trends in dogmatics have swung toward an analytic theology and are drawing upon philosophically diverse resources to enrich previous accounts of Christ's identity and mission. As a result, Torrance's theology has come in for direct critique, both in style and substance. Of particular attention is Torrance's account of the *non assumptus*. Book-length critiques by Kevin Chiarot, and essay-length discussions by Oliver Crisp and Luke Stamps, represent just three examples of theologians who have taken issue with the logical coherence and theological appropriateness of affirming the Son's assumption of a fallen human nature.[20] Meanwhile others have attempted to rehabilitate the theologumenon of the *non assumptus*, the most recent examples being myself and Jerome van Kuiken.[21]

While the debate may at first appear esoteric and peripheral, in fact much rests on the affirmation or rejection of this doctrine for how we are to understand the atonement. It is encouraging to see a number of scholars turn their attention to this aspect of Christology and bring analytical acumen to this important topic. Dan Cameron's account which follows, offers a concise dogmatic sketch of the issue, noting what is important in the debate and

18. Ibid., 53–54.

19. Ibid., 54.

20. Chiarot, *The Unassumed*. Crisp, "Did Christ Have a Fallen Human Nature?," 270–88; and Stamps, "You Asked."

21. Habets, "The Fallen Humanity of Christ," 18–44; and Van Kuiken, "The Relationship of the Fall."

where the lines of evidence might lead us. In seeking to be orthodox, evangelical, pastoral, and contemporary, Dan's account makes compelling reading and offers unique insights into the discussion. While his is not intended to be the last word on the topic, it certainly lays out the issues involved and acts as a foundation upon which further clarity around Christ's assumption of human nature might be understood. As such it fills the brief for a dogmatic sketch admirably. Might all sides of this debate further learn and penetrate this mystery of the faith.

Dr. Myk Habets

Dean of Faculty
Lecturer—Systematic Theology
Carey Baptist College & Graduate School

Preface

I WAS INTRODUCED TO T. F. Torrance's theology when I was a junior in college at Moody Bible Institute. I was drawn to his theology almost immediately. He spoke about Jesus in a way that made him real to me in a way that I had never experienced Jesus. I began to dive into his work headfirst and quickly found myself immersed into theological depth that I had never been before. It was during this time that I was introduced to the idea that Christ had assumed a fallen human nature. At first I was quickly taken aback by the notion that anything "fallen" was to be associated with Jesus. But thankfully I did not stop reading Torrance and kept trying to figure out what he was talking about.

It is critical that all who engage in theological conversation have a good understanding of dogmatic rank. Understanding that humans are fallen, this means that our logic is fallen and we do not have all of the answers to all theological questions and so dogmatic rank can help us to put theological topics in order of salvific issues and non-salvific issues. There are three parts to dogmatic rank. First rank doctrines would be doctrines that must be believed if one is a Christian. For instance, Jesus Christ being God, the Trinity, etc. Second rank doctrines would be doctrine that, while there is disagreement, those who hold varying views are still Christian but they will have separate churches. For instance, views on baptism, church government, etc. Third rank doctrines are doctrines that there may be disagreement about but all who hold them are still Christians and still worship together at the same church. For instance, tribulational views, views on creation, etc. I believe wholeheartedly that the doctrine of Christ having a "fallen" or "unfallen" nature fits in the third category. This is not a topic that we should split over but, rather, we should allow our conversations regarding this topic to sharpen us as we seek to "grow up in every way into him who is the head" (Eph 4:15). So please know that my hope in these posts is to push you to Jesus Christ and maturity in him. Let us converse in love and grace.

When you get married on of the most crucial pieces of advice that you can receive is to learn to carefully and clearly communicate with one another so as to avoid any possibility of miscommunication. I have found that, as theologians, we should take this same advice and learn to clearly and carefully communicate with each other when we speak of divine things so as to avoid any possibility of miscommunication. However, I have found this is often not the case. This book comes out of several miscommunications that I have seen concerning the nature of the humanity of Christ. In this book I do not seek to end the conversation, ending any questions that could be asked. Nor do I seek to present this as the only option to understanding the human nature of Christ. I do, however, seek to bring clarity to an already muddled conversation filled with miscommunications of various kinds.

Flesh and Blood seeks to answer the question *while remaining orthodox can it be said that Christ assumed a fallen human nature in the incarnation?* In order to accomplish this task, both sides of the argument will be examined specifically from the viewpoint of Thomas F. Torrance (fallen) and Oliver Crisp (unfallen). The first chapter introduces the reader to the discussion. The second chapter begins the inquiry by asking *what it means to say that the Divine Son assumed a fallen human nature*, giving clarification to the fallenness side of the argument. Chapter 3 continues the inquiry by asking *what are some apparent problems, which could encourage the fallenness view to be rejected*, giving clarification to the unfallen view. Chapter 4 then plays the part of mediator asking if there *is a way to retain what is helpful while avoiding the harmful consequences.* Chapter 5 closes the book by taking a look at pneumatological considerations concerning the fallen nature view.

This book could not have come to be without a lot of help from many people who I must now thank. First, to my lovely wife, Sarah, who has encouraged me and pushed me to be the best that I can and to study harder than I thought that I could and for keeping me humble when I wanted to allow knowledge to puff me up.

Second, to my mother who raised me up in the way I should go so that when I am old I would not depart from it. Thank you for pushing me even when I resisted your pushing. And thank you for standing behind me as I pursue God's calling on my life.

Third, to Dr. David Finkbeiner for the wonderful years spent being his TA and for the priceless opportunities that he has given me. To Dr. John Clark and Dr. Marcus Johnson, thank you for introducing me to the theology of T. F. Torrance and showing me what it is like to do theology well. Thank you for helping me fall in love with God even more through the beauty of theology.

Finally, so those who gave feedback, edited, and encouraged me along the way. Dr. David Luy and Dr. Tom McCall, for helping me bring this project to fruition. To Dr. Jerome Van Kuiken, and Dr. Gary Deddo for your editing, feedback, and encouragement to me all along the way. To Dr. Myk Habets, thank you for your feedback and contribution to this work.

Chapter 1

Setting the Stage

"For that which he has not assumed he has not healed;
but that which is united to his Godhead is also saved."

GREGORY OF NAZINANZUS

I WAS AT CHURCH recently and we were in the middle of our time of musical worship when we began singing a song that most people are probably familiar with, "Jesus Messiah" by Chris Tomlin. The lyrics began, "He became sin, who knew no sin, that we might become his righteousness."[1] Tomlin is quoting 2 Corinthians 5:21. When I have heard this verse explained it is usually in the context of defending the sinlessness of Christ, which I am a fan of, but I don't recall ever addressing "he became sin." I do believe that this is because we like to look over the things that we don't quickly understand, or the things for which there is not an easy answer. Sadly, I think that this topic has become one of the topics that we ignore because it is a hard topic without an easy answer. In a recent conversation I had with a friend about this after I explained what this book would be about he asked me this question, "Do I need to know this to get into heaven?" Of course the answer to this question is no, but should that stop us from trying to understand it? The answer to that question should be an emphatic no! In theology it can be hard to hold the tension between doctrines such as the full deity of Christ and his full humanity. I believe that we have

1. Tomlin, "Jesus Messiah."

become so afraid of those that wish to make Jesus out to be simply a man,[2] we have lost sight of the reality that he was truly man just like us and his humanity has an important part to play in our atonement and it is not purely for the sake of mortality. So I ask, in what ways, and using what language, must we speak of the "flesh" of Jesus Christ? This is a question that many have sought to answer. It is a question that we must discuss so that we do not fall into Docetism or Nestorianism, etc. This also raises the question of the status of his human nature. Is it fallen, like the status of our nature currently, or is it unfallen, similar to that of Adam before the fall? This is a question has seemingly been on the forefront of current theological conversation. Luke Stamps has spoken of this topic for the Gospel Coalition as recently as 2012.[3] Oliver Crisp published an article in the *International Journal of Systematic Theology* in 2003 on this topic.[4] Kelly Kapic wrote an article in the *IJST* in 2001.[5] Ian McFarland, in 2008, published an article for *IJST* as well.[6] This is not simply a recent conversation though, as there is a section in the Monthly record of the Free Church of Scotland in 1984 entitled "Did Christ have a Fallen Human Nature?"[7] To which T. F. Torrance responded through a letter to the editor.[8]

Those who want to affirm that Christ assumed a fallen human nature "are often interpreted as sacrificing the sinlessness of Jesus,"[9] and thus sinners still need a savior. On the other side of the debate, those who want to affirm an unfallen human nature are often accused of presenting a Jesus who is not "truly man, thus losing the soteriological significance of his life, death, resurrection

2. Here I am thinking specifically of the quest for the historical Jesus.

3. Stamps, "You Asked."

4. Crisp, "Did Christ Have a Fallen Human Nature?," 270–88.

5. Kapic, "The Son's Assumption," 154–66.

6. McFarland, "Fallen or Unfallen?," 399–415.

7. Macleod, "Did Christ Have a Fallen Human Nature?," 51–53.

8. Torrance, "Letter to the Editor," 114.

9. Kapic, "The Son's Assumption," 154.

and ascension."[10] It is a debate that needs much clarity if we desire to move forward at all.[11]

This brings me to the purpose and significance of this project. First, the discussion of the full humanity of Christ has been the topic of discussion for centuries, even leading to the demise of those who held what was considered unorthodox. This study is an attempt to work towards a better understanding of the full humanity of Christ. Second, I desire to show that there are arguments that can answer some of the problems proposed by defenders of the unfallen camp. Third, I hope to bring additional clarity to the discussion and put this discussion in its rightful category within dogmatic rank.

In order to accomplish the above purposes I will be using the theology of two of the main proponents of the debate, Oliver Crisp (unfallen) and T. F. Torrance (fallen). I will attempt to exposit the doctrine as held by these two theologians creating a sort of theological dialogue between the two theologians.

Why did I choose Crisp? I was reading Crisp's article "Did Christ Have a Fallen Human Nature?"[12] and the first and most obvious reason that I chose him is that he has this article and a few other writings specifically on the topic of Christ's assumption of a fallen or unfallen human nature.

The second reason that I chose Crisp has to do with T. F. Torrance. In the above named article, Dr. Crisp attempts to make an argument for Christ's assumption of an unfallen human nature while arguing against those who hold that he assumed a fallen human nature. He names Karl Barth, James Torrance, Edward Irving, etc. but does not give mention to T. F. Torrance. Since James Torrance has only published one book and T. F. Torrance has published many more, many that have to deal precisely with this topic,

10. Ibid.

11. One thing that points out the necessity of clarity is the very fact that some are referring to the debate as "fallen vs. unfallen" and others refer to it as "fallen vs. sinless" view. The very use of different terms for the conversation immediately causes confusion in the mind of the outside reader.

12. Crisp, "Did Christ Have a Fallen Human Nature?".

I thought it unfair that James Torrance gets treatment while the more prolific T. F. Torrance is not even mentioned. Instead of using an already existing argument, Dr. Crisp creates his own version of an argument for fallenness in order to show its shortcomings ultimately declaring the fallenness argument invalid and unorthodox. He claims, "any such candidate argument has to overcome apparently insuperable difficulties posed by this view, difficulties to do with the fact that fallenness requires original sin."[13]

My third reason in choosing Dr. Crisp is to take this statement as a challenge to see if there is a candidate argument that can overcome the difficulties posed. Since T. F. Torrance was not addressed by Crisp, I am using his argument as the candidate argument.

The fourth reason that I chose Crisp is his statement that the argument he proposed *for* the fallenness view "appears to be fatally flawed if one wishes to retain a Chalcedonian Christology."[14] He attempts to achieve this in three stages. First, he looks at the "theological problem original sin poses for defenders of the fallenness view."[15] Second, he attempts to propose what he says is "one version of the fallenness view that seems, *prima facie*, to overcome these problems."[16] And third, he takes his Augustinian understanding of original sin and applies it "to the argument in defence of the fallenness view, outlined in the second stage."[17] For Dr. Crisp, fallenness implies original sin and the original sin implies guilt and to get around this so that fallenness could be affirmed "original guilt needs to be exercised from original sin."[18] In order to understand Dr. Crisp's argument with clarity, his understanding of original sin must be understood and subjected to careful examination.

Now comes the question about why I chose Dr. T. F. Torrance. The first reason is a reason that I have already mentioned.

13. Ibid., 288.
14. Ibid.
15. Ibid, 271.
16. Ibid.
17. Ibid.
18. Ibid, 278.

Torrance is rarely mentioned in Dr. Crisp's writings. Alister Mc-Grath notes that it will be clear that "the time has come to explore the ideas for which Torrance established his reputation as one of the most productive, creative and important theologians of the twentieth century,"[19] and Paul Molnar notes that Torrance is "one of the most significant English-speaking theologians of the twentieth century,"[20] and as such, he has a prevalent voice in this debate and it seems unfair to not give his argument a fair trial. When Dr. Luke Stamps mentions this debate he calls this a "live issue among contemporary theologians following in the footsteps of Karl Barth and *T. F. Torrance.*"[21] Torrance is recognized, as a prevalent voice in this debate and therefore, part of my project will give space to allow Torrance to be heard in response to the critiques of Dr. Crisp.

I hope, secondly, that this project will help to create a greater awareness of this theological giant. Torrance has hundreds of publications and lectures that are a treasure trove of theological genius that I believe can greatly assist the modern theologian in our theological endeavours.

Thirdly, this is an attempt to clarify what exactly Torrance means when he says that Christ assumed a fallen human nature. Dr. Jerome Van Kuiken, in his doctoral thesis, helpfully points out the slew of possible interpretations of Torrance. Various interpretations of "fallen nature" ranging from Christ "experiencing sorrow, physical weakness, and solidarity with others' conflict with God whilst himself remaining at peace with God,[22] to Christ carried original sin and an 'evil inclination' in his flesh throughout his early life until it was condemned and slain with Christ himself as Calvary."[23] Duncan Rankin has even noted apparent Apollinarian tendencies in Torrance's earlier theology that shifts in his later

---

19. McGrath, *T. F. Torrance*, 107.

20. Molnar, *Thomas F. Torrance*, 1.

21. Stamps, "You Asked," emphasis mine.

22. Kang, "Concept of the Vicarious Humanity."

23. These interpretations found in Van Kuiken, "The Relationship of the Fall," 48–49.

theology.[24] It will thus be necessary to give an analysis of Torrance's early and later theology in order to gain a complete understanding of what Torrance is saying and where the shift takes place so that we can be clear on where he stands on the issue and so that the dialogue I will create between Dr. Crisp's theology and Torrance's theology is not only clear but is also fair.

In order to accomplish the task above, my project will be set up in such a way that I can answer the overarching question: *while remaining orthodox, can it be said that Christ assumed a fallen human nature in the incarnation?* In order to answer this question I will have three main chapters answering three sub-questions. Chapter 1 will seek to answer the question *what does it mean to say that the divine Son assumed a fallen human nature, and why might it be helpful to confess such a thing,* with T. F. Torrance as the main proponent of the "fallen" side. Chapter 2 will seek to answer the sub question, *what are some apparent problems which could encourage such a view to be rejected,* with Dr. Oliver Crisp as the main proponent of the "unfallen" side. Chapter 3 will seek to answer the question, *is there a way to retain what is helpful while avoiding the harmful consequences?* This chapter will play the part of mediator between the two sides in an attempt at clarity. Chapter 4 closes out this book with a look into the pneumatological considerations concerning the fallen nature view.

Before this projects moves forward any more I have to take a moment to put this topic in its place in dogmatic rank. By dogmatic rank I mean the three tier ranking system for the importance of theological issues. The first rank doctrines would be things that we would consider someone not a Christian if they rejected them (i.e., the deity of Christ, etc). The second tier are topics that we would still consider someone a Christian even if they reject them but we will most likely have different churches over these issues (mode of baptism, views on the Lord's supper, etc.). The third tier would be doctrines that we can disagree on, still consider someone a Christian even if they reject it, and we will still worship together

---

24. Rankin, "Carnal Union."

(i.e., views of creation, most eschatological views, etc.).[25] Far too often theological conversations can turn volatile quickly. I have seen people stop being friends over the Calvinism vs. Arminianism debate. As theologians we must have a healthy understanding of the dogmatic ranking system so that our conversations can be more productive. Now while I believe this conversation to be important and I think that we should have a stance on the issue, this conversation belongs in the third tier. It is an issue that we should engage with and in but we must realize that we can still worship with those on the other side of the issue from us. Let us keep this in mind as we move forward.

25. This system is from my lectures in systematic theology that I had with Dr. John Feinberg, Dr. Lisa Sung, and Dr. Kevin Vanhoozer. I am thankful to them for reiterating the importance of this system in all three classes.

Chapter 2

Understanding the Fallen Nature View

". . . The creation of Jesus in the womb of the Virgin presupposes the first creation, and betokens a recreation in the midst of and out of the old. That is a large part of the significance of the Incarnation, That Christ really comes to us, to our flesh and assumes it; that out of our fallen humanity which God has come in Christ to redeem and reconcile fallen sinful human beings to himself, he created and assumed flesh for himself for ever, to be one with it."

THOMAS FORSYTH TORRANCE

Introduction

As WITH ANY THEOLOGICAL debate, if we are not as clear as possible in our exposition and declaration of our views they can to more damage than good. In the debate over Christ's humanity, I believe, this is what has happened. We have no seemingly clear explanation of what it means that Christ assumed a fallen human nature. Does it mean that Christ merely experienced the external effects of a fallen nature (mortality, etc.), or does it mean something more than that? Does it mean that Christ assumed sin so that he himself became tainted? You can see why we need clarity, since that is the easiest conclusion one could draw simply from the words "Christ assumed a fallen human nature." In an attempt to be very clear in my articulation of the fallenness position, as called for by Crisp, this chapter seeks to answer the question *what does it mean to say that the divine Son assumed a fallen nature, and why might it be helpful to confess such a thing?* This will be addressed through two possible interpretations of T. F. Torrance's theology, a weak view and a strong view of fallenness. The weak view comes from Torrance's earlier theology found in his lectures at Auburn found in the book *The Doctrine of Jesus Christ: The Auburn Lectures 1938/39*, and the strong view from his more mature theology found in his lectures at Edinburgh found in his books *Incarnation* and *Atonement*. In an attempt to provide the most clarity, this chapter will give two plausible ways of understanding the "fallenness" view. The first will be fallenness that does *not* entail the assumption of original sin, and the second will be fallenness that *does* entail the assumption of original sin. These ways of understanding the fallenness view will serve the greater purpose of helping us to understand *if we can say that Christ assumed a fallen nature while remaining orthodox.*[1]

Theological Groundwork

Before I explain these two possible understandings of the fallenness view there is some groundwork that must be laid first. The virgin birth must be discussed, for it "establishes the reality of Jesus' humanity."[2] And the theological reality of the homoousion must be discussed for it shows that "in Jesus Christ, God and man, divine and human nature, are indissolubly united in one incarnate person, so that the whole of Christ's life from beginning to end was lived in unbroken relation with God the Father."[3] We can, and must, look to the revelation that has been given us to search and

---

1. This is the main question that my whole project seeks to answer through the examination of the three sub-questions already discussed in my introduction.

2. Chiarot, *The Unassumed*, 96.

3. Torrance, *Preaching Christ Today*, 58.

discover something of the reason for, and the way in which, Christ came to earth.

When the topic of the virgin birth arises, the answer to why it was necessary, I have found, is often "*so that* he could die*.*" This, I believe, misses the point of the virgin birth, and it shows that, as Torrance says, we "presuppose from the start that there is nothing more here than normal biological process."[4] To ask this is to ask the question of, specifically, *how* Christ entered this world, which is "really quite beyond our knowing."[5] This is why we must be careful not to speak of the virgin birth in merely biological terms, for in asking "biological questions of the Virgin birth you will get biological answers."[6] We must begin to ask the theological questions of the virgin birth, for the virgin birth ultimately "points to the secret of Christ's person"[7] and to the "mystery of the hypostatic union."[8] The doctrine of the virgin birth tells us three incredibly critical things concerning the person of Christ and the hypostatic union.

First, *the virgin birth grounds the true humanity of Christ.* Scripture shows us that Jesus was "really born of Mary, born through all the embryonic processes of the womb as other human beings."[9] Thus, the virgin birth "means that neither Ebionite nor Docetic Christologies are in place."[10] It is important however to note the difference between Christ and us. Though Christ was born in the "same flesh as our flesh," the birth of Christ was a monergistic movement of grace by God for he was not born "as other

---

4. Torrance, "The Doctrine of the Virgin Birth," *15*.

5. Torrance, *The Doctrine of Jesus Christ*, 108.

6. Ibid.

7. Ibid, 116.

8. Chiarot, *The Unassumed*, 95.

9. Torrance, *The Doctrine of the Virgin Birth*, 18.

10. Torrance, *The Doctrine of Jesus Christ*, 116. Torrance also states, "Can we likewise hold the 'Very God and Very Man' truth of the incarnation without lapsinf into either Ebionitism or Docetism, apart from the Womb of the Virgin?" (ibid.).

men are of the will of the flesh." [11] While the virgin birth does show that Jesus was born differently than all other men (he was born of a virgin by the will of God and we are born of the will of man) it "really conveys the idea that Jesus was a genuine man." [12]

Second, *the virgin birth reveals the divine origin of Christ.* For Christ was not born as the rest of us were, he was born of the Spirit as a creative act of the Father. Philippians 2:5 says that Christ "emptied" himself. This can be a misleading term, however, for it could be taken to mean that Christ emptied out all, or even part, of the divine attributes when he came to earth. However, we should think of this as a "veiling of his divine nature." [13] And that which was veiled in the incarnation becomes unveiled in the resurrection. We will come back to this concept in just a little bit. And so we can think of the kenosis in this way; Christ "emptying," it is not an emptying of "something" out of himself like water out of a pitcher. Rather, we could say that Christ "emptied *himself* out of heaven on to earth, out of Eternity into time." [14] For, if Christ emptied anything out of himself, if he lost any part of his divine attributes at all, he would cease to be fully God and if he is not fully God we have to question whether he is God at all. And "unless very God himself is there in Christ, unless the whole of heaven is in Jesus of Nazareth, we cannot be saved by him. For salvation has to do with God, very God." [15]

Third, *the virgin birth betokens a fracture in the sinful autonomy of humanity.* For the first time since Adam fell a man was born not of the will of sinful man. While Jesus has continuity with us, in our humanity, [16] he has discontinuity with us for he was "true

---

11. Torrance, *Incarnation*, 100.

12. Torrance, *The Doctrine of Jesus Christ*, 118.

13. Ibid, 110.

14. Ibid.

15. Ibid, 111.

16. At this point it is not necessary to discuss whether this continuity is a fallen continuity or not. What is important is to show that there has to be an aspect of discontinuity with us in order for him to be our Savior.

Son of God in true union with the Father."[17] And out of a sinner, Mary, by a pure act of God on account of his grace and love, Jesus is born and, in resisting sin, he sanctifies what "sin had corrupted" and unites it again to "the purity of God."[18] While we must say that our acts are tainted with sin and sin permeates to the depths of our very being, we must think of "sinful acts as excluded in the birth of Jesus Christ."[19] To put it another way "remembering the nature of sin, as the act of human assertion over against God is entirely excluded."[20] We must confess, therefore, that the incarnation is an atoning incarnation.

It is in light of Christ's discontinuity with us in his union with the Father that we must now turn our attention to the *homoousion*. At the Council of Nicea the term that was decided upon to describe the consubstantial relationship of the Father and Son was *homoousios*. It is this idea that is of "staggering significance"[21] for it expresses "the heart and substance of our Christian faith."[22]

The homoousion can be said to have an ontological significance. In this ontological significance we must affirm that what God is in himself, he is in Jesus Christ towards us. For "what kind of God would we have, then, if Jesus Christ were not the self-revelation or self-communication of God, if God were not inherently and eternally in his own being what the Gospel tells us he is in Jesus Christ."[23] The ontological significance of the homoousion tells us that there is oneness in *being* and *action* between Jesus and God. Who God is, Jesus is. What God does, Jesus does. Who God is outside of time in eternity, Jesus is in time and space. We can know without a doubt that when we look into the face of Jesus we look into the face of God. If Jesus were not in perfect oneness with God then we have no salvation. "For it is in virtue of his Deity that

17. Torrance, *Incarnation*, 94.

18. Ibid, 100.

19. Torrance, *The Doctrine of Jesus Christ*, 119.

20. Ibid.

21. Torrance, *The Ground and Grammar*, 160.

22. Torrance, "The Evangelical Significance," 165.

23. Torrance, *The Trinitarian Faith*, 134.

his saving work as man has its validity."[24] It is God uniting himself to our humanity that we become one with God. This is a doctrine of intrinsic relations or "onto-relations."[25] Elmer Coyler puts it so well,

> The *homoousion* is vital, for if the homoousial bond between Jesus Christ and God is cut, the bottom falls out of the gospel, because only God can atone for sin and save. Yet it is also critical that Jesus Christ is of one and the same being and nature with humanity, for if the incarnate Son is not fully human, the gospel is also emptied of soteriological significance.[26]

In this ontological aspect of the homoousion it must also be confessed that Jesus Christ is the mediator between God and man. One method that is often taught as a way to explain the gospel to someone is to draw a picture of a huge canyon. On one side of the canyon all of us stand in all our sin and guilt. This sin and guilt separates us from God, who is on the other side of the canyon. But when you get to Jesus you draw a picture of the cross creating a bridge to God. Now while this method falls theological flat in several places, it does show that Christ had to step into the situation to join us back with God. But this method makes Jesus look like a third party who simply gets used instrumentally so that we can cross over to God and never have to look back. It would be more accurate to say that Jesus Christ had to step into an intense situation of conflict between "the covenant faithfulness of God and the unfaithfulness of man and took the conflict into his own flesh as the incarnate Son and bore it to the very end."[27] It is here that we see the atonement beginning to take place before the cross. The atonement is part of the whole life and death and resurrection of

24. Torrance, *The Mediation of Christ*, 54–55.

25. Torrance, *Reality and Evangelical Theology*, 42–43. "Generally speaking, what is meant by 'onto-relation' is the kind of relation subsisting between things which is an essential constituent of their being, and without which they would not be what they are" (ibid.).

26. Coyler, *How to Read T. F. Torrance*, 81.

27. Torrance, "Atonement and the Oneness of the Church," 251.

Christ and it is not a third party that stands in for us so that we can get to God. Rather, God himself in the Son stood in the gap. Jesus, "the Just in the place of the unjust stood under judgment and rendered to God the answer of complete obedience, even to the death of the Cross."[28]

The homoousion, the "internal relation of Christ to the being of the Father,"[29] is "inseparably bound up with the hypostatic union,"[30] that is, "the internal relation of the atonement of the incarnate Person of Christ."[31] We must not and can not make a dichotomy between the "life and acts of Christ."[32] The incarnation is not merely a "prelude" to or simply "necessary means for atonement."[33] Rather the incarnation and atonement are inseparable in the very being and actions of Jesus Christ as the God-man. At the heart of the hypostatic union we are taught that Jesus Christ is both God and man, both divine and human, united so as to never be unbroken within one incarnate person so that the entire life of Christ was lived in perfect and unbroken relationship between Christ and his Father. This means that his person and work cannot be separated and "his humanity is not just a means to an end."[34] This being the case, atonement and reconciliation should be thought of as taking place "within the incarnate constitution of the Mediator. His person and work are one . . . Jesus Christ *is* redemption, he *is* righteousness, he *is* life eternal."[35] Therefore, the incarnation and atonement must be thought of in terms of their "*internal* relations within the incarnate constitution of Christ."[36]

Having laid the foundation of the nature of the divinity and humanity of Christ and the relationship between the two as

28. Torrance, *Conflict and Agreement*, 245.

29. Torrance, *The Trinitarian Faith*, 277.

30. Torrance, *Ground and Grammar*, 165.

31. Ibid.

32. Torrance, *Divine Meaning*, 263.

33. Torrance, *God and Rationality*, 63.

34. Torrance, *Preaching Christ Today*, 58.

35. Ibid.

36. Ibid., italics mine.

discussed in the doctrine of the homoousion and the hypostatic union we can now turn to two possible understandings of Christ assuming a "fallen" human nature.

Fallenness Without Original Sin

The first is an understanding of "fallenness" that does *not* entail Christ's assumption of original sin. Paul tells us that Christ came in the "likeness" of sinful flesh in Romans 8. Surely here we are faced with a great mystery. They mystery of the "relation in Person of the Holy Son of God to our fallen and sinful humanity."[37] This view says that we cannot "think of Jesus as having original sin, for his *Person* was divine."[38] Nevertheless, he really came into the sphere in which we exist and move and breathe and find our being. Jesus Christ, when incarnate, assumed "the concrete form of our human nature marked by Adam's fall,"[39] for he partook of his mother's flesh, which was "part of the Adamic race, of fallen humanity."[40] Unlike the view of Edward Irving, who states that Christ was sinless because of the indwelling Spirit, this view states that we are to think of Christ's human nature as "perfectly and completely sinless *in his own nature*, and not simply in virtue of the Spirit."[41] In order to not compromise the holiness of Jesus Christ we must confess that Jesus was "in the likeness" of sinful flesh and also "yet without sin."[42] But To understand the necessity of Christ's coming in the *likeness* of sinful flesh and yet *without* sin Torrance explains well,

> We must think of him nevertheless as really one with us, as really a member of our fallen race who is tempted in all points as we are, though without sin. Were he not really of us, he would not be our Reconciler or Redeemer or Mediator. Were he not really of us, his humanity would

37. Torrance, *The Doctrine of Jesus Christ*, 120.
38. Ibid, 122, emphasis mine.
39. Barth, *Church Dogmatics*, 1.2, 151.
40. Torrance, *The Doctrine of Jesus Christ*, 122.
41. Ibid.
42. Ibid.

be really Docetic. If he did not come to bear our sin and to be one with us sinners, he would not be our Saviour.[43]

But this can still be very confusing and does not give a very good definition of what exactly, according to this view, it means that Christ assumed a fallen human nature. Fallenness without the assumption of original sin can be defined in this way: *in the incarnation, God comes "near to sinful man, inasmuch as he was made in the likeness of sinful flesh,"*[44] *and in doing so he assumed the suffering of infirmity and temptation, the enmity of God against sin, and the enmity of Satan against sinners.* To put it the words of Torrance, *"he entered into our condemned state under divine judgment and made it his own, suffered the 'Eli, Eli, Lama sabacthani', and yielded up the Ghost under the burden of sin and judgment and wrath."*[45]

But to remain in this state would leave him in a state under judgment and disqualify him from being our savior. Instead he "condemned sin in the flesh" as Paul says in Romans 8:3. In assuming these things Christ remained sinless. "He entered *our* humanity precisely that he might so struggle with sin at close quarters and defeat it in human flesh where it had enthroned himself."[46] For the purpose of Christ becoming like us, in the concrete form of our humanity, was always for the purpose of atonement. In order to accomplish atonement, Christ *had* to remain sinless. And how can we have freedom from sin unless one who is strong enough to defeat sin and gain victory over it does it in our place? And because "sin dehumanizes, and by its entrance, the perfection of his perfect sympathy would have been irrevocably lost"[47] it must be said that he must "stand free of moral evil."[48] This is the place at which Christ stands *unlike* us. We all share in what has been

---

43. Ibid.
44. Torrance, "Predestination in Christ," 133.
45. Torrance, *The Doctrine of Jesus Christ*, 122.
46. Ibid, 123.
47. Mackintosh, *The Doctrine of the Person*, 401.
48. Torrance, *The Doctrine of Jesus Christ*, 124.

called the "mystery of personality"[49] and we all share in a personality that has been so affected by the fall that we are now masked and the reality of our personality is corrupted by the fall. But Christ, "instead of the human mystery of personality, sin, he possesses the divine mystery of personality."[50] And thus the key to his victory of temptation "must be ascribed to the presence of God in Christ." At the point where his fallen nature might result in a sinful person, we rather have the "divine person of the Logos"[51] intervening and saving the fallen human nature. Thus we can say that Christ assumed a fallen human *nature* but not a fallen human *person*. His Person was from all eternity the Son of God with his divine nature. In the incarnation he remained what he was, fully. In his fallen human nature he assumed the possibility of temptation without the *necessity* of falling prey to that temptation due to having assumed a corrupt human *person*. This is not to say that Christ does not have a human person, in an apollinarian way. But the way he has a human person is explained via the notion of *Anhypostasia*. Jesus Christ has his human person in an anhypostatic way. Torrance explains:

> Because of the assumption of humanity by the Son, Christ's human nature has its existence only in union with God, in God's existence or personal mode of being (*hypostasis*). It does *not* possess it in and for itself—hence *an-hypostasis* ("not person," i.e. no separate person).[52]

This means that apart from the divine act of grace in the incarnation Jesus Christ, "the Son of God Jesus would not have come into being."[53] There is no self-existing, independent "person" which is assumed. The person of the Son assumes a human nature and in doing so becomes personalized, has a person, by virtue of that hypostatic union. But that person is none other than the one

49. Brunner, *The Mediator*, 318.

50. Torrance, *The Doctrine of Jesus Christ*, 125.

51. Ibid.

52. Torrance, *Incarnation*, 84. Also see Torrance, "Atonement and Oneness," 249. Torrance, "The Atonement the Singularity of Christ," 230. Torrance, "The Place of Christology," 16.

53. Torrance, *Karl Barth*, 199.

person of the Son. The one person of the Son has two natures but not two persons. Thus, Anhypostasia places stress on the "general humanity of Jesus" standing in ontological solidarity with all humanity.[54] And if we are to take the Chalcedonian terms of "without confusion" seriously we must also take into account "without division and without change" seriously as well so that we don't fall into a neo-nestorianism. For "there are *not* two separate persons in Jesus Christ but one single Person. Where Christ is there is a unique undivided Person."[55]

In summary, this view states that Christ assumed a fallen human *nature*, without assuming a fallen human *person* because his person is divine.[56] This means that he was under the judgment of God and the consequences of our sin (temptation, etc.) and yet remained sinless in it. Having not sinned himself, for the act of sinning is a product of the person and not the nature, he vicariously took our place and in so doing condemned our sin in his flesh in his life, and death "sanctified the very flesh that he assumed from the virgin Mary."[57] And in his resurrection, "the last vestiges of fallenness (subjection to infirmity, mortality, temptation, and divine wrath) fall away and the new humanity which he embodies is perfected."[58] And in uniting himself vicariously to "a fallen and

54. Torrance, *Incarnation*, 230. While Torrance asserts that Jesus did not simply "adopt" a self existing person (hypostasis) he appears to have an underdeveloped doctrine of *en-hypostasis* in his early theology stressing that we must not think that Jesus' humanity "was some sort of general humanity" only. Torrance says that we cannot "let go of the idea that the Word became united to a particular man, the man Jesus of Nazareth, the historical son of Mary, who was crucified under the governorship of Pontius Pilatus in Judea, a man of definite historical record and definite historical existence, The Word became flesh, became united to an individual human being, Jesus of Nazareth" (Torrance, *The Doctrine of Jesus Christ*, 132).

55. Torrance, *The Doctrine of Jesus Christ*, 115.

56. We will return to the idea that fallen human persons *with* their fallen natures are subject to original sin and guilt because persons are guilty and natures are not.

57. Ibid., 123.

58. Van Kuiken, "The Relationship of the Fall."

accursed race under the band and wrath of God"[59] he wrought for us a *new* humanity from within our sinful humanity that gives us reason to resonate with Paul that in Christ "we are a new creation. The old has passed away. Behold, the new has come."[60]

> And in our faith we, in Christ, are hid with him in God, are assimilated to him, sinners though we are, reconciled, redeemed and recreated in Jesus, the One who is mediator between God and man, the captain of our Salvation.[61]

And we must not think of the incarnation and the atonement as two separate events, his humanity simply being the means to the end of atonement. But we must think of them as,

> Interpenetrating one another from the very beginning to the end of his oneness with us. Otherwise the humanity Christ has to be thought of only in an instrumentalist way, and the atonement has to be formulated only in terms of external moral relations or legal transactions. But if the incarnation is itself essentially redemptive and not just a means to an end, then atonement must be regarded as taking place in the ontological depths of Christ's incarnate life, in which he penetrated into the very bottom of our fallen human being and took our disobedient humanity . . . upon himself in order to heal it and convert it back to himself into union with God.[62]

Fallenness with Original Sin

There is however a second view in understanding what it means that Christ assumed a "fallen" human nature, and that is that he assumed a fallen human nature that *includes* the assumption of original sin. While I am distinctly explaining two plausible views, this does not amount to a rejection of any continuity between the

59. Ibid.

60. 1 Cor 5:17.

61. Torrance, *The Doctrine of Jesus Christ*, 123.

62. Torrance, *Preaching Christ Today*, 59.

two. For both views hold that Jesus Christ sinlessly assumed a fallen human nature and in doing so he recreated it back into the way that it was meant to be. He wrought for us a true humanity through his earthly life, in which he "experienced the progressive outworking of that sanctification through costly obedience and identification with sinners, coupled with increasing opposition not only from sinners and Satan against his holiness but also from God against his vicarious sinfulness."[63] And in this assumption of our fallenness Christ dealt with the forgiveness of our actual sins and in this view it was "original sin and original guilt that the Son of God took upon himself in incarnation and atonement, in order to heal, convert, and sanctify the human mind in himself and reconcile it to God."[64]

If we were to define what it means that Christ assumed a "fallen" human nature according to this view, we would say *that Christ sinlessly and vicariously assumed,* not only the physical consequences of sin as in the last view, *but assumes our original sin and guilt and our "twisted, distorted, bent mind," contained in our actual human nature, and in assuming it "right from the very beginning, our Lord converted it, healed it, and sanctified it in himself."*[65]

In taking from us our fallen human nature upon himself, instead of sinning as we all do, Jesus condemned sin in our carnal mind,[66] and was himself wholly without sin.[67] And so by living out a life of perfect holiness and purity in his mind, he sanctified and healed our human mind in the whole course of his incarnate and redemptive life from his birth to his crucifixion. He carried our

63. Van Kuiken, "The Relationship of the Fall," 54.

64. Torrance, *Atonement,* 440.

65. Ibid.

66. Torrance calls attention here to Romans 8:3 "For God has done what the law, weakened by the flesh, could not do. By sending his own Son in the likeness of sinful flesh and for sin,[a] he condemned sin in the flesh."

67. Torrance here calls attention to 2 Corinthians 5:21 " For our sake he made him to be sin who knew no sin, so that in him we might become the righteousness of God." And Hebrews 4:15 "For we do not have a high priest who is unable to sympathize with our weaknesses, but one who in every respect has been tempted as we are, yet without sin."

mind into the very depths of his agonizing and atoning struggle on the cross—he descended into the hell of the utmost wickedness and dereliction of the human mind under the judgment of God, in order to lay hold upon the very root of our sin and to redeem us from its stranglehold upon us.[68]

In order to understand this more fully a better understanding of the *an-hypostasis en-hypostasis* distinction must be had. We have already defined an-hypostasia as,

> Because of the assumption of humanity by the Son, Christ's human nature has its existence only in union with God, in God's existence or personal mode of being (*hypostasis*). It does *not* possess it in and for itself—hence *an-hypostasis* ("not person," i.e. no separate person).[69]

En-hypostasia makes the assertion, because the humanity of Jesus Christ is assumed by the eternal Word, that human nature is given existence "in the existence of God, and coexists in the divine existence or mode of being (*hypostasis*)—hence *en-hypostasis* ("person in," that is, real human person *in* the person of the Son)." Where an-hypostasis asserts that Jesus has a *general* humanity, en-hypostasis asserts that Jesus had real *individual* personhood, with a complete human hypostasis, "in perfect oneness with, the divine hypostasis of the Son."[70] And he did so in such a way that he did not override or diminish "the reality of the human person," but on the contrary he personalized the human nature of Christ. That is to say, he gave it en-hypostatic "reality in the Person of the Son of God become man."[71]

But what does it mean that he "personalized" the human nature of Jesus? It means that in the very moment of incarnation Christ assumed this nature, "void of an hypostasis of its own," into perfect unity with himself so that there might be "one and the same

68. Torrance, *Atonement*, 440.

69. Torrance, *Incarnation*, 84. Also see Torrance, "Atonement and Oneness," 249. Torrance, "The Atonement the Singularity of Christ," 230. Torrance, "The Place of Christology," 16.

70. Torrance, *Karl Barth*, 199.

71. Torrance, *The Trinitarian Faith*, 230.

hypostasis of the Logos and of the human nature assumed, outside of which it neither ever subsists, nor can subsist."[72] In other words, the human nature was, by itself, an-hypostatic (without personal being) and the pre-existent Logos makes this nature en-hypostatic by assuming the seed of Abraham (Heb 2:16) "as its shrine and instrument."[73] The human nature of Jesus does not and could not exist apart from the "personalizing" by the eternally existent *Logos*.

While the an- and en-hypostasia must be thought of as one movement, for they "bring out the essential logic of grace,"[74] we must understand the distinction they maintain. Because an-hypostasia states that the Logos did not assume an independently exiting *personality*, it teaches that the Logos "took possession of human nature, [so] as to set aside that which divides us men from one another, our independent centers of personality, and to assume that which unites us with one another, the possession of the same or common human nature."[75] And thus, Jesus *did not assume our fallen persons*. Within the an-hypostatic understanding of his ontological solidarity with our common fallen human *nature*, he is en-hypostatic seeking "solidarity in terms of the interaction of persons within our human and social life, in personal relations of love, commitment, responsibility, decision, etc."[76] This personalizing union has social and personal implications for in personalizing our humanity he brings about the result of the personalizing those who come into contact with him.[77] And the biggest result of this personalizing union is that "Jesus Christ is now the fount of all that is truly personal among us; we are not personal in virtue of some personal substance inherent in ourselves, but only through what we receive from Jesus Christ . . . to be personal, therefore is to be in Christ."[78]

72. Torrance, *Incarnation*, 228–29.

73. Heppe, *Reformed Dogmatics*, 428.

74. Torrance, *Theological Science*, 269.

75. Torrance, *Incarnation*, 231.

76. Ibid, 232.

77. Torrance, "The Soul and Person," 116.

78. Torrance, "The Goodness and Dignity," 318.

Our union with Christ, thus, is both physical/ontological (an-hypostatic: assumption of human nature) and noetic/personal (en-hypostatic: personalizing the human nature). So any understanding of our union with Christ that deals only with the onto-union falls short of a complete understanding of the atoning work of Christ for the union between God and man in Christ was not merely an onto-union "else there had been no cross, and the atonement had already been accomplished fully and entirely in the birth of Jesus, in the bare assumption of our human nature into oneness with the Son of God."[79]

But then the question could be asked how does this understanding of en-hypostasis help with this problem? The importance of en-hypostasia lies in a correct understanding of the personal nature of sin. For "if sin is an act of man going down to the roots of human nature and introducing into the very relation with God which constitutes the human person . . . a contradiction . . . then it is in the inner depth of their personal being that humanity must be reconciled to God and we must be healed of our enmity and contradiction to God."[80] Because the problem of sin lies at the heart, the very being of man, any act of atonement could not simply be done *to* man but rather,

> It must be worked through the heart and mind of men and women, until they are brought to acquiesce in the divine judgment on sin and are restored in heart and mind to communion with God. Reconciliation . . . is not just the clearing up of a misunderstanding, but the eliminating of a lie that has its roots in our natures as fallen and as perverted personal being. Hence the incarnation entailed a physical or ontological union, as well as a Logos-union with man (that is, a union with man in being as well as in word and mind) as the means of reconciliation to God.[81]

79. Ibid, 163.
80. Torrance, *Atonement*, 159.
81. Ibid, 158, 161.

Fallen and Atoned: Condemning Sin in the Flesh

The solution to the problem of fallenness lies at the heart of atonement. For, Christ took our fallen human nature from us "in order to redeem and recreate it in and through his incarnational assumption and atoning life and death."[82] To reject the idea that Christ did assume our postlapsarian humanity is "soteriological and evangelically defective."[83] The incarnation and atonement must not be separated. For to bifurcate the two from each other can lead to a doctrine that says that the relationship between Christ and the sinner was merely an "external, moral, legal or contractual relation."[84] So how did Christ fix the problem?

The question of how Christ condemned sin in the flesh must be discussed for this is at the very heart of *why* Christ assumed our fallen nature in the first place. The entire picture of the incarnation and atonement, Christ condemning sin in the flesh, can be summed up and thought of in two parts. First in his ontologically solidarity with us, he assumes our fallen humanity, that is human nature. It is in this solidarity with us, in the "Incarnational union of the Holy Son with our unholy nature," that we must think of Christ "dealing with our original sin."[85] It is here that our very nature, including our corrupted mind and will, is assumed and by the very act of assuming this into union with Holy God it is healed, converted, and sanctified.[86] It has been thought that this is purely the work of the Spirit in our lives post conversion but the question remains, is the Spirit working out an act of atonement separate from the person and work of Jesus Christ? Or rather is our sanctification being worked out by the Spirit only possible because our sanctification is grounded in the actions of Christ from within the depths of our fallen humanity. That is, we in our persons, with our

---

82. Torrance, "Letter to the Editor," 114.

83. Ibid.

84. Ibid.

85. Torrance, *Theology in Reconstruction*, 156.

86. Torrance, "Reconciliation of the Mind," 4–5.

natures, share by the Spirit in the perfected human nature of Jesus Christ.

The second part of the Christ condemning sin in the flesh is his life of active and passive obedience to the will of the Father. When we speak of the passive obedience of Christ what is being referred to is his submission to the "divine judgment upon us," and by his active obedience we mean that he "took our place in all our human activity before God the Father."[87] But this understanding of his active and passive obedience cannot be thought of apart from the union of the nature of God and man in the incarnation for if we do, then, a full understanding of Christ's obedience is lost and we can only think of the "justification in Christ as anything more than a merely external forensic, non-imputation of sin."[88] While the union of God and man in the virgin birth can be thought of to deal with the ontological problem of original sin,[89] it is the active and passive obedience of Christ where our *actual* sins are dealt with. Where we are disobedient, Christ is the obedient One.[90] What Christ actually did for us within our human nature be summarized like this;

> Here within our fallen and disobedient humanity [human nature], where we are less than human because of our sin, here where we have dehumanized ourselves in

87. Torrance, "The Distinctive Character," 6–7.

88. Torrance, *Incarnation*, 82.

89. The union wrought in the virgin birth deals with our original sin through bringing "it into healing and sanctifying union with his own holy nature" (Torrance, *Theology in Reconstruction*, 156). Very simply put, our actual sins are the sins that we commit, our disobedience, etc. Original sin is the ontological disease of our very being, that is, of our persons in connection with out nature.

90. "To live out in our inhumanity the life of true humanity, in the midst of our disobedience a life of obedience, and so to live the perfect life in communion with the perfect God . . . In the sheer perfection of his humanity in all its absolute purity and sinlessness he offered the Amen of Truth from within our humanity to the Word and Will of God's eternal truth . . . He stood in the gap created by man's rebellion and reconciled man to God by living the very life he lives . . . within the limitations of our humanity in the house of bondage" (Torrance, "The Atoning Obedience of Christ," 75).

our rebellion, here where we, the sons and daughters of God, have become bastards and not true sons and daughters, he the Son of God becomes true Son of Man, true man for the first time in utter obedience.[91]

It is within this corrupted nature that Christ beat his way forward back into obedience to the Father. It must be said, then, that the obedience of Christ was not a sham or something to be taken lightly. "It was agonizingly real in our flesh of sin . . ." it was "a battle."[92] Luke 2:52 says that "Jesus increased in wisdom and in stature and in favor with God and man." The word that is usually translated "increased" or "grew" can also be understood in such a way that Jesus "beat his way forward with blows."[93] His life is a movement of perfect obedience as he cuts his way forward through our alienated, fallen nature "which gathered intensity until it reached decisive enactment in the crucifixion."[94]

This is the perfect transition to now discuss what role the cross plays in Christ's assumption of our fallen human nature. Because the atonement was an incarnational atonement, the cross is the culmination of "what was taking place all the time in the incarnate life of the Son."[95] The problem of the "perversion of man's mind and attitude toward God"[96] must be dealt with in such a way that the enmity between both sides is dealt with so that there can be reconciliation and peace between God and man. It is here at the cross that sin gets its final attack at Jesus Christ but God overcomes. For "on the cross, the oneness of God and man in Christ is inserted into the midst of our being, into the midst of our sinful existence and history." And while the cross is God's judgment against us, the resurrection is his "affirmation of Jesus Christ as Son of Man and all that he has done for us in our nature."[97] And

---

91. Torrance, *Incarnation*, 73.

92. Ibid, 64.

93. Ibid.

94. Torrance, *Conflict and Agreement*, 240–41.

95. Torrance, *Incarnation*, 112.

96. Torrance, *The Doctrine of Jesus Christ*, 160.

97. Torrance, *Atonement*, 214–15.

while sin tried to break apart our union on the cross, the resurrection ensures that our union is now unbreakable, forged together even in the face of the "strain imposed through the infliction of the righteous judgment of the Father upon our rebellious humanity which Christ has made his own."[98] And at the cross we see humanity's final attempt at rejecting God, and we see God's final rejection of humanity's sin. And as Christ bears this divine rejection in his very person he does so in such a way as to "slay the old sinful and perverted adamic existence."[99]

Conclusion

In this chapter, two versions of Christ assuming a fallen human nature have been set forth from the perspective of T. F. Torrance. The first, weak view is an assumption of a fallen human nature that does *not* include the assumption of original sin. Fallenness without the assumption of original sin can be defined in this way: *in the incarnation, God comes "near to sinful man, inasmuch as he was made in the likeness of sinful flesh,"*[100] *and in doing so he assumed the suffering of infirmity and temptation, the enmity of God against sin, and the enmity of Satan against sinners.* To put it in the words of Torrance, *"he entered into our condemned state under divine judgment and made it his own, suffered the 'Eli, Eli, Lama sabacthani', and yielded up the Ghost under the burden of sin and judgment and wrath."*[101]

The second, strong view is an assumption of fallen human nature can be defined such *that Christ sinlessly and vicariously assumed,* not only the physical consequences of sin as in the last view, *but assumes our original sin and guilt and our "twisted, distorted, bent mind,"* contained in our actual human nature, and in

---

98. Ibid, 216.
99. Ibid, 132.
100. Torrance, "Predestination in Christ," 133.
101. Torrance, *The Doctrine of Jesus Christ,* 122.

assuming it "right from the very beginning, our Lord converted it,
healed it, and sanctified it in himself."[102]

Torrance was not being inconsistent in his theology by having two differing views on this topic, but rather, his earlier theology (the weak view) matured into his strong view as laid out in this chapter. The two views are, therefore, not contradictory, but complementary with the later being a more developed understanding of the former with an emphasis on the external condition and the later on the state of our ontological corruption.[103]

I recognize that this chapter lacks interaction with the problems that some have raised with this view and I ask for you patience, as we will come to them in the following chapters. But, I close this chapter with a summary quote from Torrance addressing the foundational reason why Jesus Christ assumed our fallen human nature,

> In Jesus Christ the Son of God entered into our rebellious humanity laid hold of the human nature which we had alienated from the Father in disobedience and sin, and by living our from within it the life of perfectly obedient son, he bent our human nature back to the obedience of the Father. Standing in our place, in life and death, not only to be questioned but to give a faithful and true answer, he answered for us to God; even in his terrible descent into our God-forsakenness in which he plumbed the deepest depths of our estrangement and antagonism, he reconstructed and altered the existence of man, by yielding himself in perfect love and trust to the Father. "Father into thy hands I commend my spirit." "Father" had been the answer of his whole life on earth, the answer of the obedient son, for through the whole course of his obedience from birth to death he bent our human nature back into a perfectly filial relation of faith and truth toward the Father. "Not my will, but thine be done."
>
> And the Father answered the cry of his Son from the depths, answered not in word only but in deed, answered

102. Ibid.

103. For more on this, see Van Kuiken, "The Relationship of the Fall."

by resurrecting Jesus from the dead as his own Son with whom he kept faith and truth even in the midst of judgment and death. "Thou art my beloved Son." But that is the answer that God directs to us all in the Gospel for Jesus' sake, that through Jesus the Son of God became our brother, we may be restored to faith and trust in the heavenly Father. Through sharing brotherhood with the incarnate Son of God, we share with him also one and the same Father Almighty.[104]

104. Torrance, *Theology in Reconstruction*, 125–26.

Chapter 3

Is Fallenness a Problem?

". . . No substantive meaning can be given to the notion of 'fallenness' that does not entail sinfulness, even in some weak, non-culpable form. All of which appear to be fatal to the fallenness view."

OLIVER CRISP

Introduction

WHILE TWO PLAUSIBLE UNDERSTANDINGS of the fallenness view have been set forth, it must be understood that there are more than one side to an argument. Conversation swirling around the atonement, more specifically the nature of the atonement, brings its own level of volatility into these conversations. This is because the "nature of the atonement—how it is that Christ's life and death on the cross actually atone for human sin—remains a theological conundrum,"[1] and thus, we must hear the arguments against the fallenness view in order to gain clarity as we seek to understand the truth. Many have charged that, and agree with Dr. Crisp that, it is *not* "possible to make logical sense of the notion that Christ's humanity was fallen."[2] Dr. Crisp speaks of the debate as follows: the fallenness view vs. the sinlessness view (the unfallen side). He

1. Crisp, "Original Sin and Atonement," 430.
2. Crisp, "Did Christ have a Fallen Human Nature?," 270.

argues that the fallenness view must be rejected on the grounds that Christ was sinless.[3] Although he rejects the fallenness view, he admits that Christ may have been *affected* by the fall for he experienced sorrow, hunger, etc. But, as Kelly Kapic has noted, because there has been a lack of clarity concerning this topic,[4] this chapter looks at objections, making use of Crisp's argument with more depth. We will deal with potentially serious problems for defenders of the fallenness view; problems that may put those defenders in theologically murky waters. The goal of this chapter is to answer the question *what are some apparent problems, which could weight against the fallenness view?* In order to accomplish this, the doctrine of original sin will be examined more closely to see if and how a traditional Augustinian understanding of this doctrine poses problems for the fallenness view. Those who hold the fallenness view maintain that Christ sinlessly assumed a fallen human nature. But is this a viable conclusion to come to? No, according to Crisp, on the following basis: "Not if fallenness requires sinfulness. This is the issue upon which the fallenness view stands or falls."[5] Addressing this claim will be followed up with an attempt to make "logical sense of the notion that Christ's humanity was fallen."[6] And in closing, this potential argument (against the fallenness view) will be put to the test to see if it stands of falls prey to orthodoxy.

---

3. Crisp, *Divinity and Humanity*, xi.

4. "We must conclude by demonstrating that the issues at hand are less clear than sometimes acknowledged, requiring more than simply an affirmation of wether the Son assumes a *fallen or unfallen* nature. Given the lack of clear and agreed definitions, claiming one position or the other does not actually convey much of theological substance" (Kapic, "The Son's Assumption," 163–64).

5. Crisp, "Did Christ have a Fallen Human Nature?," 286.

6. Ibid, 270.

Essentially Human

There are those that, having read the arguments of those on the fallen side, have deduced several possible reasons for holding to the fallenness view. One motivation seems to be that Christ had to have a fallen human nature so that the incarnation could be meaningful and not some abstract event asking the specific question, which I believe is representative of the general critique, "how could Christ really be like us except that he assume, not some abstract condition, but the concrete (and therefore fallen) condition in which we find ourselves?"[7] This point argues, simply put, that fallenness is essential to being fully human as we are fully human. To deny this is to deny that Christ is fully human and to undermine the reality of his atoning work that must regenerate our human natures if we are to take our fallenness with full seriousness.

But the question must be asked, what are essential human properties that one must have in order to be fully human? For Adam was fully human before the fall (yet lacking fallenness). Following Crisp, we can say that there is a distinction to be made between *contingent* and *essential* properties of human nature. Contingent properties are those properties of an individual human that are not necessarily shared by all other humans for contingent properties may be gained or lost. This would include things such as "having a right arm, or possessing a good memory, etc."[8] And, whereas contingent properties are not properties necessarily shared amongst all humans, essential properties are properties that cannot be lost while the person remains "the same concrete individual."[9] That is,

7. Stamps, "You Asked." Commenting on Karl Barth's argument that "There must be no weakening or obscuring of the saving truth that the nature which God assumed in Christ is identical with our nature as we see it in the light of the fall. If it were otherwise, how could Christ be really like us? What concern would we have with him? We stand before God characterized by the fall. God's son not only assumed our nature but he entered the concrete form of our nature, under which we stand before God as men damned and lost" (Barth, *Church Dogmatics* 1.2, 153).

8. Crisp, "Did Christ have a Fallen Human Nature?," 272.

9. Ibid.

if an essential property is lost the person is no longer the same individual that they once were. Essential properties could be things such as "having a particular soul, having a particular parentage, or having a particular genetic code."[10] And at the same time, it is very possible that there may be properties "which happen to be *common* to members of a natural kind, and which may even be *universal* to all members of that kind, without being *essential* to membership in the kind."[11] So while contingent properties can be universal and appear to be essential they are not. According to the point just made, the property of "fallenness" "is not an *essential* property of a particular human nature."[12] In other words, "fallenness" is not a property that is essential for one to posses in order to be fully human. This should be an uncontroversial claim for no one thinks that pre-lapsarian Adam was less than fully human, and since at least two humans (Adam and Eve) did not possess the property of fallenness, at least for a time, fallenness is not an *essential* property.[13] According to this logic then, and in line with opponents of the fallen nature view, Christ did not need to assume the contingent property of fallenness in order to be "fully" human.

How then can we think of the human nature of Christ? According to Crisp, the nature of Christ existed as *anyhypostasis physis*, that is, "a human nature that exists independently of an individual *hypostasis*."[14] That is to say, the human nature has no existence as a person apart from its assumption by the Word. Another way to think of this is to say that the nature assumed by the Word, though "never a person as such (independent of the Word),

---

10. Ibid.

11. Morris, *Our Idea of God*, 164.

12. Crisp, "Did Christ have a Fallen Human Nature?," 272. This is a point raised by Morris as well in *The Logic of God Incarnate*, ch. 3.

13. While we say that Adam was fully human before the fall it could be argued that post-lapsarian humanity is in a sense *less* than human for we now live in a state other than the state in which we were created to be in. But this is another topic for another time.

14. Crisp, *Divinity and Humanity*, 72.

exists 'in' the *hypostasis* or person of the Word and is thereby personalized (that is, *hypostazised*) by the Word."[15]

Crisp, holding to a concrete understanding of human nature,[16] believes that the human nature of Christ has no existence apart from the incarnation and the assumption of that nature by the Word. His nature becomes personalized upon assumption. And to take it a step further, the only reason that Christ's human nature even exists at all "is the virginal conception brought about by the Holy Spirit."[17] But this nature does not simply have a certain set of universal properties but rather possesses a certain set of concrete properties. In the case of Christ it can be said that he did have those "properties common to all human beings (a kind essence) as well as other properties that are particular to Christ's humanity, such as being born in Bethlehem in a manger, being in hypostatic union with the Word of God, and so forth."[18] But the question may be asked, how does one who holds to the concrete particular view understand the an-enhypostatic distinction? One way is to say that the anhypostatic nature of Christ "has those properties that are common to all human beings . . . And these properties exist independently of the Incarnation."[19] So in a real way, according to anhypostasis, one can affirm the universal properties exhibited by Christ's human nature that exist independently of the particular nature of Christ. But what makes this view different from some "abstract-nature views" is that Christ does not merely have some universal properties. "Rather, what we should say is that he has a

15. Ibid, 72–73.

16. This view, according to Oliver Crisp in his book *Divinity and Humanity*, 49, says, "(1) Human natures do not exist independently of human beings. (Human natures are concrete particulars).

(2) Christ has a human nature in addition to a divine nature.

(3) The human nature of Christ exists because the Holy Spirit brings it into being.

(4) This human nature of Christ does not exist independently of the theanthropic person of Christ."

17. Ibid, 80.

18. Ibid, 81.

19. Ibid. 81–82.

human body and human soul distinct from the Word that form a concrete particular that is his human nature."[20] What follows from this is that Christ's nature, while anhypostatic it is also enhypostatic. "That is, it exists only 'in' the person of the Word."[21] Christ takes the unpersonalized human nature, which could not be assumed by anyone but the Word, and upon assuming it in the incarnation he literally "personalizes" it. Crisp puts it this way,

> The Word is fully a person "prior" to the Incarnation. At the Incarnation he assumes the body-soul composite that is the natural endowment of a human being, which, in the case of other humans, would be sufficient to constitute a human person, but which does not do so in the case of Christ because the Word assumes it instead, thereby "personalizing" it. Thus, it is the Word who is the logical subject of the body-soul composite that makes up his human nature. They are *his* human soul and body, and thereafter could not be the body and soul of any other person, because they have no existence independent of the Word from the first moment of the Incarnation onwards.[22]

And,

> In the case of the Incarnation, this means that the concrete particular that is the human nature of Christ is "personalized" through the hypostatic union with the Word, thereby preserving the enhypostatic aspect of the *an-enhypostatic* distinction. It is also the case that if the three-part Christologist is realist about properties, some sense can be made of the claim that Christ's human nature is anhypostatic. Christ has those properties common to all human beings, as well as those properties particular to Christ alone, and these properties are universal. Nevertheless, it is the concrete particular that is Christ's human nature that has these properties.[23]

20. Ibid, 82.
21. Ibid.
22. Ibid, 83.
23. Ibid, 89.

Crisp, in making the case that Christ an- and enhypostatically has a human nature the property of fallenness was not yet discussed but must be. For the sake of our his argument, he assumes "that Christ has a fallen human nature"[24] as we exposit the doctrine of original sin and then apply that understanding to Christ in an attempt to make sense of the 'fallenness' view in light of the Augustinian understanding of original sin.

The Problem of Original Sin

In order to understand how the traditional doctrine of original sin may cause problems for the fallenness view, we must have a clear understanding of original sin. Simply understood, original sin is composed of two parts original *guilt* and original *corruption*. This was thought, by medieval theologians, to have been an *inherited* trait from our parents. Though, as Oliver Crisp notes, those in the Reformed tradition maintain that guilt and corruption were "directly, or immediately *imputed* to all of Adam's posterity after the fall."[25] It was not, however, imparted by means of natural generation it was simply imputed to everyone.[26] For the sake of this argument when original guilt and original corruption are referred to it will be thought of as imputed.

Original corruption "involves a propensity or proneness to actual sin, but it is not the same as actual sin."[27] An example would be one's proneness to drink too much alcohol when offered a drink so as to get drunk but this is not the same thing as *actually* getting drunk. This does not necessitate, *prima facie*, that one will, without a doubt, sin. But Augustinian theologians take this further and say that humans *will* inevitably sin while remaining in the state of corrupt without divine intervention.[28] At the very least, Crisp says, we

24. Crisp, "Did Christ have a Fallen Human Nature?," 273.

25. Ibid.

26. Crisp notes that this is only the case for those not in the Saumur School of Reformed theology, following Placaeus.

27. Ibid, 274.

28. This point is made by Swinburne in *Responsibility and Atonement*,

must say that this propensity to sin, as with a disease, will manifest itself at "some point in their lives . . .and with such proneness will (probably) sin on at least one occasion,"[29] especially without the presence of divine intervention.

On the flip side of the coin of original sin we find original guilt. While original corruption is the stain on our very being that gives us the *propensity* to sin, original guilt is the "culpability aspect of guilt that accrues to Adam's first sin."[30] In other words, Adam's guilt is imputed to us so that we are now culpable and guilty before God. But some have, more recently, began to question the notion that we are guilty of Adam's sin. One such theologian is Oliver Crisp who argues that the "problem with it is that guilt is not a notion that admits of transfer from one person to another. Whereas punishment may be transferred, guilt may not."[31] Here is an example to illustrate this point. I was on my way back to Chicago from Dallas one summer. The speed limit for most of the way from Dallas to Illinois at the time was 75 so I had my cruise control set at 83. When I crossed into Illinois the speed limit changed from 75 to 70 and within a mile of crossing into Illinois a state trooper pulled me over for now going 13 miles over the speed limit. I was given a $220 speeding ticket as a punishment for what I had done wrong. Now suppose that I did not have enough money to pay the fine for myself but my friend Ryan had the $220 necessary to pay the fine and paid it for me. In that case, I am at once free from the punishment for my crime. Although my fine was paid, my guilt was not erased. And no matter what Ryan does there is no way that he can absorb my guilt. He can only pay my punishment. This seems to clearly show that guilt is non-transferable.[32]

Although guilt is seemingly non-transferable some have made the distinction between liability to guilt and liability to punishment. Liability to guilt is non-transferable for it lies at the

---

138.

29. Crisp, "Did Christ have a Fallen Human Nature?," 274.

30. Crisp, "Original Sin and Atonement," 437.

31. Crisp, "Did Christ have a Fallen Human Nature?," 274.

32. Wainwright, "Original Sin," 31–60.

essence of their sin even though God may have forgiven them for their sin. And liability to punishment is transferable because it relates to penal sanction and not the essence of sin. In other words, what is meant by liability to punishment,

> Is desert of punishment, or obligation to render satisfaction to God's justice for self-determined violation of the law. Guilt in this sense is not of the essence of sin, but is rather a relation to the penal sanction of the law. If there had been no sanction attached to the disregard of moral relations, every departure from the law would have been sin, but would not have involved liability to punishment. Guilt in this sense may be removed by the satisfaction of justice, either personally or vicariously. It may be transferred from one person to another, or assumed by one person for another.[33]

Ryan could pay my actual punishment for me, freeing me from my punishment. But I am, in a sense, also freed from my guilt for it would be unjust to punish me twice for one crime.[34] This view of imputed guilt is known as *immediate* imputed guilt, not to be confused with *mediate* imputed guilt. Immediate imputation of guilt could be described like this "all human beings post-fall have imputed to them Adam's guilt, and, as a consequence of this, Adam's corruption."[35] It is important to recognize the distinction between liability to punishment, which seems to be a logical consequence to liability to guilt, and liability to guilt.

So while the classic Reformed doctrine of original sin is comprised of both corruption and guilt, we seem to run into a problem of transference. While the purpose of this chapter is not to solve the problem of how guilt may be transferred from Adam to us "it

33. Berkhof, *Systematic Theology*, 246.

34. "A man condemned at a human tribunal for any offence against the community, when he has endured the penalty which the law prescribes, is no less unworthy, his demerit as much exists as it did from the beginning; but his liability to justice or obligation to the penalty of the law, in other words, his guilt in that sense of the word, is removed. It would be unjust to punish him a second time for that offence" (Hodge, *Systematic Theology*, 2:189).

35. Crisp, "Did Christ have a Fallen Human Nature?," 278.

may be conducive to our concerns with Christ's fallen humanity" since, if a possible understanding of sin without original guilt can be had in the case of Christ's human nature then, according to Oliver Crisp, there may be "grounds for an argument in favor of the notion of Christ's fallen humanity."[36] But before we can examine whether the traditional Reformed doctrine of original sin causes a problem for those who advocate for the fallenness view even if a revision needs to be made (removing original guilt),[37] the question that must be asked is simply this: *"does possession of original corruption, even in the absence of original guilt, mean that the person in possession of such a condition is damned?"*[38] In other words, does the very possession of corruption, aside from being guilty of any actual sin, still make one stand before God condemned for corruption? Oliver Crisp answers this yes. "For God could refuse such an individual a place in heaven even where he never actually sins, or has original guilt, merely because, in virtue of having a *fallen human nature (original corruption)*, he is loathsome to God and must have the blessings of heaven withheld from him."[39] So even if a person was free from actual sin, but in possession of original corruption, that person would still be in a place of fallenness and thus damned. Thus, Crisp argues, that according to "Reformed orthodoxy . . . being fallen entails being sinful," for "possession of original corruption is itself a sin."[40] At the very least to be fallen has to include the possession of original corruption. Thus if fallenness does require sinfulness then according to this view, "This is the issue upon which the fallenness view stands or falls."[41] But, aiming at fairness, Dr. Crisp attempts to set forth an argument for the fallenness view with these things in mind and with a revision

36. Ibid, 278–79.

37. Ibid, 279.

38. Ibid.

39. Ibid., emphasis mine. Note Crisp's definition of the fallenness view: that is possession of original corruption.

40. Ibid, 280.

41. Ibid, 286.

of the "Reformed doctrine" of original sin. We must now turn to examine his argument.

Revising Original Sin

Crisp argues that in order to have a possible orthodox understanding of Christ having a fallen human nature, the "traditional doctrine of original sin"[42] must be revised to make logical sense of this idea of Christ's fallenness. The argument that he makes has fourteen premises. We will now look at those in turn.

(1) It must be said that the Son of God, the Second Person of the Trinity "elects to take himself a human nature."[43] That is, the Word chose to enter into space and time as the man Jesus Christ. (2) The nature that the Word once assumed must be said to have an individual essence. The man Jesus has no existence apart from the personalizing of the Word. (3) This nature that has individual essence is of the kind, human being. Jesus Christ's human nature is of the same essence as all other human beings (this is not a reference to fallen or unfallen characteristics). (4) Not only does this nature have its existence only in the Word and not only is this essence of the same kind as us, the human nature of Jesus Christ is "fully, but not merely, human."[44] To be fully human is to be, simply put, human plus. To be merely human is to be human and nothing more (like all of us). So we can say that Jesus was *fully* human, but as the Son of God he was not *merely* human due to the hypostatic union of the divine nature of the Word.[45] (5) This truly/fully human nature of Christ is "one of two natures held in hypostatic union in the person of Christ."[46] According to the Chalcedonian definition;

---

42. Ibid, 280.

43. Ibid.

44. Ibid.

45. This is discussed in more detail in Morris, *The Logic of God Incarnate*.

46. Crisp, "Did Christ have a Fallen Human Nature?," 280.

> Two Natures unconfusedly, unchangeably, indivisibly, inseparably; the difference of the Natures being in no way removed because of the Union, but rather the properties of each Nature being preserved, and (both) concurring into One Person and One Hypostasis; not as though He were parted or divided into Two Persons, but One and the Self-same Son and Only-begotten God, Word, Lord, Jesus Christ; even as from the beginning the prophets have taught concerning Him, and as the Lord Jesus Christ Himself hath taught us, and as the Symbol of the Fathers hath handed down to us.[47]

In the first five premises the humanity of the man Jesus Christ as the God man has been established. Now the sixth premise has to do with the state of that human nature. (6) The human nature of Jesus Christ has the properties of fallenness. (7) The reason that this is a true premise is because "the property of 'being fallen' is a contingent property of *all* human natures after the fall of Adam, without exception."[48] This, of course, is in reference to the human natures that exist currently on earth that have not yet been transformed into glory, as distinguished from those united to Christ by faith whose human natures are being transformed through divine intervention. Thus, without divine intervention all human beings exist in a state that can be called "fallen." Since all post-lapsarian human natures exist in the state of fallenness, (8) the human nature of Jesus Christ is fallen. As argued earlier in this paper no sense can be made of "fallenness" if it does not entail original sin thus, (9) Christ's fallenness means that he has original sin. (10) And if Christ has original sin then he has to have "inherited corruption and inherited guilt."[49] (11) This then means that if Christ does have original sin (as in 9 and 10) as with the rest of humanity then Christ is "thereby culpable."[50]

---

47. "The Definition of Faith," from session 6 of the Council of Chalcedon. See Tanner, *Decrees of the Ecumenical Councils*, 86.

48. Crisp, "Did Christ have a Fallen Human Nature?," 281.

49. Ibid.

50. Ibid.

why wouldn't God make Jesus from the dust of the Earth? Why be born into the corrupt human race?

Premise 11 is the heart of the problem for Dr. Crisp and thus it is at this point that a revision would be necessary in order to secure an understanding of Christ's fallenness that does not require sinfulness and so avoid the violation of christological orthodoxy regarding Christ's sinlessness. But as they stand, these premises embody the classical understanding of inherited original sin which when "coupled with a commitment to a 'fallenness' doctrine of Christ's humanity, yields the conclusion that Christ's 'fallen' human nature is sinful."[51]

Crisp offers a variation of this argument, starting after point (9),[52] which stated that Christ's fallenness meant that he assumed original sin. The variation begins at (10) which now states that though Christ has original sin this "does not entail that Christ is *guilty* of being sinful."[53] (11) For, Christ could have original sin without original guilt. Crisp maintains that while original guilt may or may not make sense, a defense of the "fallenness" view simply needs to say that original corruption needs to be transferred to the human nature of Christ without original guilt, (12) in which case it can be said that Christ's human nature is fallen which means that he possess original corruption but not original guilt.

According to Crisp, there are two possible understandings of original corruption that involve the strength of that corruption within you. The first is "weak" original corruption which says that "human beings post-fall actually sin because of original corruption."[54] The other is "strong" original corruption which states that "humans beings post-fall inevitably actually sin because of original corruption, without the prevenient grace of God."[55] If

---

51. Ibid, 282.

52. Crisp claims "None of the defenders of a fallenness doctrine of Christ's humanity that I have read would affirm this proposition, for the very reason that it commits them to the claim that Christ is sinful, which is clearly unorthodox" (ibid.). As seen from chapter 1, at least in Torrance's more mature writings (Edinburgh Lectures) he seems to be arguing that Christ does assume our original sin so as to deal with it "in the flesh" Romans 8:3.

53. Ibid.

54. Crisp, *Divinity and Humanity*, 109.

55. Ibid.

"strong" corruption was the case for Christ, it would seem that he would inevitably sin and thus no longer be our savior. But the "weak" view does not say that actually sinning is inevitable but rather is a consequence of being corrupt (but not a necessary consequence). Therefore, those defending the fallen view may "endorse a weaker view of inherited corruption, taking as concomitant to this view the idea that Christ's fallen human nature is . . . (*posse peccare*)."[56] Although it is possible that Christ could have sinned on at least one occasion, the divine grace that was upon him enabled him to resist actually sinning. Thus (13) Christ's *human nature* may actually sin. But, (14) due to divine grace, is prevented from ever actually sinning.

What has just been laid out is one potential argument for the fallenness view according to Dr. Crisp. However, this argument leaves him wanting and he sees several problems with this argument.

First, "on this argument Christ would be sinful."[57] I agree with Crisp that if an argument leads to the conclusion that Christ is sinful, we have a huge problem. To say that our Lord is sinful means that we are not saved for he did not fix anything; rather he became tainted by his own actual sins. Scripture definitely tells us a different story. Second Corinthians 5:21 says that although Christ "became sin" he "knew no sin," he committed no act of sin himself. For he was the spotless Lamb of God who came to take away the sins of the world! According to Crisp, "this alone is fatal to the fallenness view."[58]

Second, Crisp objects, "even if Christ has original corruption and not original guilt, this means that his human nature is vitiated, and . . . loathsome in the sight of God."[59] Original corruption would mean that Christ has some sort of deformity, as each of us do, and this deformity would then render him loathsome in God's sight and thus incapable of being our Savior! "So, the argument

56. Crisp, "Did Christ have a Fallen Human Nature?," 283.
57. Ibid, 284.
58. Ibid.
59. Ibid.

folds once again, for the same reason as before: it is theologically unorthodox."[60]

Third, "Christ cannot commit actual sin."[61] Based on the understanding of original corruption set forth by Crisp, even if one is corrupt but not guilty, that person will sin at least once without divine intervention (assuming the strong view of corruption). But if Christ was to sin then we are in real theological trouble. Thus it must be said that Christ did not commit actual sin. However, Crisp notes, "But this is one of the principal reasons for endorsing the fallenness view,"[62] and if Christ's sinning is not possible then Crisp asks, why hold the fallenness view in the first place?

Because the charge was brought against the fallenness view that argues that there is no plausible argument for the fallenness view that elimates the possibility of Christ's sinning, we must now examine this idea of Christ's ability to sin or not to sin in a little further detail.[63] This idea of ability to sin or not to sin is helpfully understood in the categories set forth for us by St. Augustine in his *posse peccare* model.[64] Thomas Morris sets forth one explanation for the *posse non peccare* understanding of Christ's nature. That is, Christ is able *not* to sin. He uses the example of a person entering a room that has a two hour timed lock on the door. The person in the room is unaware of the two hour timed lock and so is unaware that, even if they chose to leave the room, they would be unable to leave because of the lock. This person remains in the room the entire two hours unaware of her inability to leave the room. But a few minutes after the lock disengages, she chooses to leave the room unaware of the lock. In this sense, she is still responsible for not having left the room even though she would have been prevented

---

60. Ibid.

61. Ibid, 284.

62. Ibid.

63. For a deeper discussion on the difference between what Crisp calls the sinless and impeccability views see Crisp, *God Incarnate*, 122–36.

64. Simply put this model is fourfold. Able to sin (*posse peccare*), Able not to sin (*posse non peccare*), Not able not to sin (*non posse non peccare*), and finally not able to sin (*non posse peccare*).

anyways. In the same way it is meaningful to claim *posse non peccare* in Christ's case, for, Christ never chose to sin even though if he did choose to do so the divine nature would have prevented it from ever happening.[65] But to claim that Christ is able not to sin is different than claiming that Christ is able *to* sin (*posse peccare*). Crisp believes then that on this view, (*posse peccare*), Christ would have sinned on at least on occasion. Thus, Morris, arguing along the same lines as Crisp, says "it is not possible, on this view, that Christ's humanity successfully resists every temptation without the intervention of divine grace (either Christ's divine nature or the Holy Spirit)."[66]

In building upon the analogy set forth by Thomas Morris, if the person in the room is prevented from leaving the room by electrodes in her brain that are being controlled from an adjacent room by some scientist then it is not the person who resists going out the door but rather the scientist. In the same way if Christ is simply prevented from sinning it is not his human nature that is resisting but rather the divine nature overriding the human nature. Thus it can be said that "Christ's humanity is *able to sin*, being fallen, yet is prevented from sinning by divine intervention."[67]

And while this seems to be a logical way of understanding his sinlessness, according to Crisp, "it poses problems for defenders of the fallenness view."[68] For if one of the main reasons for holding to the fallenness view is to say that he is able to sin so as to make sense of the temptations, if Christ is prevented from sinning by the divine nature or the Holy Spirit then in reality he is actually unable to sin due to the intervention of divine grace. Thus, "one of the reasons for endorsing the fallenness view, namely, that Christ is truly tempted, and truly resists temptation by his (fallen) human

---

65. Morris, *The Logic of God Incarnate*, 150. Morris also draws from the work of Frankfurt, *The Importance*.

66. Crisp, "Did Christ Have a Fallen Human Nature?," 286.

67. Ibid., emphasis mine.

68. Ibid.

nature alone, is removed."[69] And, this being the case, Christ is not *posse peccare* but rather, *non posse peccare.*

Here is where Crisp's argument really falls apart. He is viewing Christ's nature as something that is capable of existing "alone." It seems to be the case that we can say that Christ's humanity, on its own, is indeed *posse peccare* if he did in fact assume a fallen nature. The problem is that his nature, and ours as a matter of fact, was and is never meant to be alone. To approach Torrance's theology with this type of "aloneness thesis"[70] is a serious misunderstanding of Torrance's theology. To do that is to critique his theology using a method Torrance never used to come to any conclusions. Deddo argues that the problem with this "aloneness" approach is that our "Western habits of mind almost inevitably regard relationship as extrinsic, as accidental to who and what God God's creation and creatures are." Deddo continues, "Everything that can be said to have being is essentially what it is without being related to anything else."[71] In other words, nothing exists in a vacuum; everything exists in relation to other. We were always meant to have our being in relationship. All the benefits of our salvation were never meant to be benefits that could be had apart from Christ. Rather, we only have these benefits in relationship with Jesus. Thus, using this same "onto-relational," as Torrance calls it, methodology, Jesus' human nature can and must never be understood or talked about apart from his divine nature and person. Crisp and Morris both approach this conversation from a non-onto-relational methodology and thus misunderstand what Torrance is trying to say and how he gets to the conclusions that he comes to.

Conclusion

What has been set forth in this chapter is an argument against the fallenness view. In keeping with my original question, *what are*

69. Ibid.

70. Thank you to Dr. Deddo for pointing this problem out to me!

71. Deddo, "The Realist," 121.

some apparent problems, which could encourage the fallenness view to be rejected, some great questions and apparent problems have been raised by Dr. Crisp that must be dealt with in the chapter to follow in order to help us make some sense of this whole debate. According to Crisp "if fallenness requires sinfulness" then the fallenness view must be rejected for this is "the issue upon which the fallenness view stands or falls."[72] And through an examination of the doctrine of original sin, his argument that even the very presence of original corruption (even if one can have corruption without guilt) would leave one standing loathsome in the sight of God has shown, according to him, that "since fallenness requires sinfulness of some sort, no sense can be made of the fallenness view along these lines."[73] And his only solution to this, if one wants to maintain that Christ had a fallen human nature, is to revise the doctrine of original sin (which he has shown to be unsuccessful) or abandon Chalcedonian Christology. According to this argument, then, "defenders of the fallenness view do not appear able to articulate a version of the doctrine that is orthodox, even if they can make sense of original corruption without original guilt."[74] Crisp points out that this does not mean that no sense can be made of being sinless/unfallen while being affected by the effects of the fall. He points out the argument of Augustine,

> God could of course have taken a man to himself from somewhere else . . . not from the race of Adam who had implicated the human race in his own sin . . . But God judged it better to take a man to himself from the very race that had been conquered, in order through him to conquer the enemy of the human race; to take one however whose conception from a virgin was inaugurated by the spirit not the flesh, by faith not lust
> What was born, I say, was a man who had not and never would have any sin at all, a man by whom would

72. Ibid.
73. Ibid, 286–87.
74. Ibid.

be reborn all those who were to be set free from sin, who could not themselves be born without sin.[75]

This idea of unfallen/sinless and yet affected by the consequences of the fall is present in the theology of Augustine and this can make sense of passages where Christ is tired, weak, sad, etc. "So he has the propensity to physical, and perhaps moral, weakness. But exemplifying the effects of the fall in his human nature is not the same as possessing a fallen human nature . . ."[76] Crisp explains this with a thought experiment. Imagine a regime that could produce the symptoms of measles in someone without actually having the bacteria. They would have all the symptoms such as the spots, fever, etc. but never have the actual disease. In this way "Christ possessed the symptoms of sinful humanity in terms of moral and physical weakness, without possessing a sinful human nature that gives rise to these effects. In this sense then, Christ takes on the infirmities of a fallen human nature, but did not take on the condition of fallenness."[77] And thus the unfallen/sinless view (juxtaposed to the fallenness view) is able to make sense of Christ's identification with fallen humanity without himself being fallen.[78]

While Crisp says that he has "not claimed that there is no other argument that may be mounted in defense of the fallenness view," he continues, ". . . any such candidate argument has to overcome apparently insuperable difficulties posed by this view, difficulties to do with the fact that fallenness requires original sin."[79]

Dr. Luke Stamps also raises issue with the fallenness view for four reasons which we should consider.

First, he claims that the fallenness view "tends to neglect the fact that fallenness is not intrinsic to humanity."[80] So fallenness

---

75. Augustine, *The Trinity*, 361–62.

76. Crisp, "Did Christ have a Fallen Human Nature?," 287.

77. Ibid, 287–88.

78. Ibid, 288.

79. Ibid.

80. Stamps, "You Asked."

is not part of humanity that must be healed. For "fallenness" is a condition of "moral corruption and a propensity towards sin."[81] And for Christ to have a real and genuine incarnation and in order to complete his vicarious work, is for him to assume a *full* human nature (body and soul) rather than a *fallen* human nature. For it is apparent that Adam was truly and fully human before he fell, thus fallenness is not intrinsic to being fully human.

Second, the fallenness view "assumes that one can be in a state of fallenness and not be sinful."[82] Here Stamps resonates with Dr. Crisp in saying that the "mainstream Reformed understanding of original sin argues precisely the opposite: to possess a fallen nature is to be guilty before God."[83]

Third, the fallenness view seems "to pose serious challenges to the historic understanding of the person of Christ."[84] But if Christ assumed a fallen human nature how could Christ, being infallible and the Son of God, be joined to a "morally fallen human nature?"[85] In order to get around this would we need to affirm that the Son is not impeccable, or that there are two persons in Christ? Stamps believes that these things to be avoidable only if the fallenness view itself is avoided.

Fourth and finally, the fallenness view seems to "ignore the fact that we can affirm what might be called the fallen experience of Jesus without positing a fallen nature to him."[86] What this means is that we can speak of Christ truly experiencing the effects of the fallen nature without having the fallen nature. This experience would include his hunger, tiredness, sorrow, his weeping in Gethsemane, etc. "We are not to imagine that Christ blissfully waltzed through life untrammeled by the suffering, sorrows, and

81. Ibid.
82. Ibid.
83. Ibid.
84. Ibid.
85. Ibid.
86. Ibid.

pains of fallen human experience."[87] And thus none of his work must be surrendered in rejecting the fallenness view.

Both these arguments raise some questions that must be looked into juxtaposed the fallenness view that I have set forth in chapter 1, especially since Crisp makes little to no reference to T. F. Torrance at all.[88] And thus, we turn to the third chapter to examine these first two chapters (that is the fallenness argument and the problems that Crisp raises) to see if there is a way that we can move forward in this debate with clarity. As Kelly Kapic asks, "What language should one use to describe the nature assumed by the Son? Why do the least excitable Christians turn instantly into the most passionate debaters when the discussion of whether or not the Son assumed a *fallen* or *unfallen* human nature arises?"[89] While both sides of this debate (fallen vs. unfallen) "think nothing less than the very heart of the gospel is in jeopardy,"[90] we will attempt to move forward with charity. Kelly Kapic, in his article "The Son's Assumption of a Human Nature: A Call for Clarity," wisely helps us understand that while those who seek to affirm the fallenness side are "often interpreted as sacrificing the sinlessness of Jesus," on the other side those who defend the unfallen nature "are often charged with presenting a generic Jesus who is not truly man,"[91] we must find a way to move forward charitably as we work together to come to a fuller understanding of Jesus Christ as understood in Scripture.

87. Ibid.

88. In his chapter and article on "Did Christ have a Fallen Human Nature" Crisp has one footnote to James Torrance and the only footnote with T. F. Torrance's name, which is simply a citation of Karl Barth's *Church Dogmatics* that Torrance helped translate.

89. Kapic, "The Son's Assumption," 145.

90. Ibid.

91. Ibid.

Chapter 4

Searching for Answers

"What language should be used to describe the nature assumed by the Son? Why do the least excitable Christians turn instantly into the most passionate debaters when the discussion of whether or not the Son assumed a fallen or unfallen human nature arises? Professional theologians, pastors and lay people quickly become impassioned because of what they believe is at stake."[1]

KELLY KAPIC

Introduction

So FAR I HAVE presented two possible ways of understanding what it means to say that Christ assumed a fallen human nature and I have presented some of the reasons why it may be unhelpful and potentially unorthodox to claim such a thing. This chapter will seek to answer the question, *is there a way to retain what is helpful while avoiding the harmful consequences?* In order to accomplish this task, this chapter will address the four main issues raised against the fallenness argument. We will then take a look at how pneumatology may help this conversation. And one thing

1. Kapic, "The Son's Assumption," 154.

that appeared to be lacking in both the fallen and unfallen arguments is an analysis of Scripture and thus the second part of this chapter will take an examination of the main texts of Scripture that address this issue. One very critical piece in this debate that *must* have more clarification is a solid definition of *nature* vs *person*. This chapter will continue with another potential argument for the fallenness side that takes into account the issues that were raised in chapter 2. And finally this chapter will conclude by taking a look at the things that we can confess with surety while recapping the whole of the project.

Addressing the Issues

The first issue that will be addressed here is the idea that "no sense can be made of this fallenness view"[2] if fallenness is equal to sinfulness and the very possession of corruption makes one loathsome in the sight of God. Crisp maintains that God must refuse an individual who is corrupt a place in heaven, even if they never actually sin but they still have guilt, "merely because, in virtue of having a *fallen human nature* (original corruption), he is loathsome to God and must have the blessings of heaven withheld from him."[3] He continues that according to Reformed theology the very possession of corruption is itself a sin. Crisp is right to say that if Christ is sinful (if fallenness is equal to sinfulness) then the fallenness view has huge problems and must be rejected for on this basis Christ would not be the spotless lamb who has come to take away the sins of the world. We must confess "Christ is an exception to the anthropological rule that 'all have sinned and fall short of the glory of God.'"[4] However, I believe that Crisp's argument here is lacking on the grounds of the relation between "nature" and "hypostasis" and how they relate to the concept of "fallen" and "sinful." Far too often sin has come to be thought of as simply man's

2. Crisp, *Divinity and Humanity*, 114–15.
3. Crisp, "Did Christ have a Fallen Human Nature?," 279, emphasis mine.
4. McFarland, "Fallen or Unfallen?," 400.

"moral deviation from God's will" and as such "it is not surprising that they have rejected the idea that Christ's identification with the human condition includes participation in sin."[5] In other words if fallenness is a "symptom of sinfulness,"[6] then of course it makes sense to reject that Christ was fallen since, on this logic, for Christ to be fallen means that what came first was his sinfulness. But if our willing follows our desire then the "reason that human beings sin is that there desires are perverse. But when it comes to explaining *why* those desires are perverse, the only answer that can be given is, 'Because we are sinners'—that is, in terms of the 'whoness' . . . that is the mark of a created nature with a will."[7] Thus, the will is a feature of the nature where our "status as agent is revealed" and "discloses a limit to my ability to account for my being solely in terms of my whatness."[8]

The counsel of Chalcedon (AD 451) defined the whole being of Christ as true God and true man united, without confusion, division, separation, and without change in the one hypostasis of the Second Person of the Trinity (The Son of God). He is consubstantial with the Father and also with us. And if we were to apply the logic in the above paragraph to Christ rather than us we see that "the fact that his hypostasis (i.e. *who* he is) is the second person of the Trinity and thus divine means that things come out differently."[9] In order for Christ to be our savior there must be a point of discontinuity with us as well as point of continuity. The discontinuity is that "while we sin because we are sinners, Christ does not sin because, as the divine Word (i.e. hypostasis of the Trinity), he is not a sinner."[10] To speak of Christ's will as deified is to speak in terms of his operation as a person in human nature. For instance, where our wills are sinful and thus turned away from God, "Christ's will is at every point turned toward God, so that

5. Ibid.
6. Ibid.
7. Ibid, 411.
8. Ibid.
9. Ibid.
10. Ibid.

his willing is shaped by God's will for him."[11] While this is a point of discontinuity with us, it is only discontinuity in relationship toward God and not in basic ontology of will. Thus we can say based on this logic that sin is characteristic of hypostasis rather than nature. Thus, Christ can assume a fallen human nature and remain sinless. Ian McFarland rightly says,

> Because Christ's sinlessness is in this way a function of hypostasis and not of his human nature, the fact that his will was deified says nothing about the character of the rest of his nature and does not constitute a conceptual obstacle to the idea that he assumed a fallen human nature. Nor, contrariwise, does the assumption that the human nature he assumed was fallen imply that he was sinful—*even on an Augustinian understanding of original sin.* This is because sinfulness—as a perversion of the created will—is properly attributed to hypostasis rather than to nature. For while the will is formally a property of human nature, its material content as fallen is a function of the disposition of the I—and thus of hypostasis.[12]

Even though our fallen wills are thus because of the indivisibility of person and nature ("so that if the former is fallen, the latter is sinful").[13] Christ is exempt from this because his person pre-exists as the eternal Word of God and thus his person is not bound by his human nature due to his "eternal subsistence in the divine nature."[14] We can confess, then, that fallenness is not equal to sinfulness for "fallenness is a property of nature and sin of hypostasis. A nature can be damaged (and thus fallen); but a nature cannot sin, because sin is ascribed to agents, and thus is a matter of the hypostasia."[15] Crisp said that possession of a fallen human nature, that only has original corruption, is still loathsome in the

---

11. Ibid, 411–12.

12. Ibid, 412.

13. Ibid.

14. Ibid.

15. Ibid. 412–13. McFarland points out that this "damage to nature" is (e.g., the body's corruptibility).

sight of God, but if fallenness is an attribute of hypostasia then we must first rethink the language of sinful *nature* and secondly no matter how "damaged" a nature is (however you would define damaged nature, as long as that damage does not entail sinfulness) a nature cannot be morally evil and must remain good.[16] Thus "our nature never separates us from God."[17] Christ can, thus, have a fallen human *nature* and this does not call orthodoxy into question. For "The condition of fallenness is attributable only to the nature, not to the acting person [of Christ]."[18] If fallen human nature was equal to sinful human nature then Crisp's logic is correct because Christ would be sinful and we would be left needing a Savior. But if, as argued above, sinfulness is the ontological state of our hypostasis (person) and we thus morally deviate from God's will on the ground of the corruption of our person, then, due to Christ's person being that of the Second Person of the Trinity, Christ could be said to have a fallen human *nature* and yet remain sinless and Crisp's logic argument falls flat on the basis of attributing corruption (and guilt) to nature rather than person. As Torrance says it is in solidarity with man that the "Incarnational union of the Holy Son with our unholy nature," that we must think of Christ "dealing with our original sin."[19] And it is here that our corrupted mind and will is assumed, and in the very act of assuming our fallen nature with its corrupt and carnal mind he healed, converted, and sanctified it.[20] This is only plausible on the grounds of a *vicarious*[21] assumption. It is never *his* corruption or *his* guilt; it is always *our* corruption and *our* guilt.

16. McFarland notes that "even a nature so damaged as to be 'fallen' remains good and not evil" (ibid., 413).

17. Ibid. "In this way, we sin *because* we are already sinners; but because our sinfulness if logically prior to our acting as agents, our agency is not the cause of our sin. Instead, our sinfulness turns out to be deeper than those individual acts of the will for which guilt and blame may well be appropriate responses."

18. Sumner, "Fallenness and Anhypostasis," 212.

19. Torrance, *Theology in Reconstruction*, 156.

20. Torrance, "Reconciliation of the Mind," 4–5.

21. By vicarious I mean, done in the place of another.

The second issue that will be addressed here is the idea that, according to Crisp, since one of the main reasons for holding the fallenness view is to say that Christ could have sinned makes no sense, and thus, the fallenness view should be called into question. I have yet to read anyone from the fallenness side of the debate (i.e., T. F. Torrance, James Torrance, Karl Barth, Edward Irving, etc.) who state that they hold to the fallenness view so as to make sense of the temptations and say that Christ could have sinned. Crisp is right to say that Christ is incapable of committing actual sin for that would compromise the integrity of the very ontological person of God. Thus, since the bent toward sin and the very possibility of committing sin is to be attributed to hypostasis rather than nature, we can maintain that Christ was sinless. But as Karl Barth argues he was not sinless because he lacked concupiscence of because he was *non posse peccare* but because he was *obedient* to the Father. Unlike us, who are determined to recommit the sin of Adam daily due to the corruption of our person in union with fallenness of nature, Christ takes on our flesh to sanctify it "nevertheless, the reality of a sanctified life was a fight, not just a being. Jesus had to obey. But it was a fight that could not have had another result."[22] While Crisp says that those in the fallenness camp want to maintain that Christ was *posse peccare* it is clear that Barth speaks, differently but similarly, that Christ is impeccable on the grounds of his active and passive obedience rather than on the Augustinian grounds of *non posse peccare*. For "sin is not necessary for Jesus, even in his fallen humanity, because it is not necessary for us either."[23] For us to sin is to act out of our bondage of the will[24] but Christ approaches his life in true freedom as the Son of God and as such to choose to sin was "excluded from his choice of acts. In virtue of his being, he was unable to choose it. Therefore he did not choose it. And he did not do it."[25] And as Karl Barth says,

22. Barth, *Table Talk*, 69.

23. Sumner, "Fallenness and Anhypostasis," 205.

24. See Luther, *Bondage of the Will*.

25. Sumner, "Fallenness and Anyhpostasis," 205–6. See also McFarland, "Willing Is not Choosing," 3–23.

> Thus the man Jesus does not transcend the limits of the
> humanity common to Him and us, or become alien to
> us, when in His acceptance of human essence even in
> its perversion he does not repeat the perversion or do
> wrong, when in virtue of His origin He cannot will or
> do it. He is just what we are and how we are. The only
> difference is that he is it in genuine human freedom. If
> he takes to himself the contradiction of our essence, it is
> only to overcome and resolve it.[26]

So, while Crisp says that those on the fallen side want to hold
that Christ is not impeccable, from the example of Barth we see
that they do hold to impeccability but on different grounds than
Crisp.

The third issue that will be addressed here is that, again according to Crisp, another reason for holding the fallenness view is
so that one can say that Jesus was *fully* human, but fallenness is not
an intrinsic characteristic to be fully human the fallenness view,
thus it should be called into question once again. Crisp is right to
say that in order for Christ to be fully human he did not need to
assume a fallen human nature. Fallenness is not necessary for one
to be fully human. If this was the case then Adam before the fall
was not fully human. But while Crisp is right to confess this, he is
missing the point of Christ assuming a fallen human nature. As
can be seen from the first chapter, Christ's assumption of a fallen
human nature is not about being *fully* human but rather about
atonement of fallen human beings. And so Crisp is right and yet is
wrong to say that this is a death blow to the fallenness view for the
fallenness view is arguing in terms of atonement and not fullness
of being human or mere solidarity with humanity.

The fourth issue that will be addressed here is the question of
how could God be a holy God and yet be joined to a fallen nature
in Jesus Christ? Luke Stamps poses the question this way, the fallenness view

> would seem to pose serious challenges to the historic
> understanding of the person of Christ. According to the

26. Barth, *Church Dogmatics*, IV/2, 93.

"Definition" issued at the Council of Chalcedon, there are two distinct but inseparable natures (divine and human) *hypostatically* (that is, personally) united in the one person of the Son. But how could the infallible Son of God be joined to a morally fallen human nature? Would this not call into question the divine Son's impeccability, that is, his inability to commit sin? Or would one need to posit two persons in Christ, and hence the heresy of Nestorianism, in order to preserve both the impeccability of the Son and the fallenness of Jesus Christ?[27]

For Stamps the only solution is the abandonment of the fallenness view completely. But, as has already been argued, Christ can be said to be impeccable and yet have a fallen human nature. For to be corrupt and sinful, again, is characteristic of person and not nature. But if you take the view that Christ also assumed *our* corrupt and carnal mind he could do so without compromising who he is as God because he did not leave it there! The very nature of God and man being united is a healing union. I think of the women who touched the cloak of Jesus and by the very touching of a disease-ridden women with Jesus Christ healing took place. In the same way when the fallen human nature comes into contact with the divine, healing takes place. Stamps says that the solution is to abandon the fallenness view or to believe in Nestorianism, but as I have argued this is not the only solution.

A question that must be raised concerns the first definition of fallenness without original sin. Torrance argues that Christ assumed the *suffering of infirmity and temptation, the enmity of God against sin, and the enmity of Satan against sinners*. The question that must be asked is how the suffering of infirmity and temptation is a post-lapsarian consequence. It appears as though Adam was tempted before he ate of the fruit and as this seems to be the case how can we say that this is a "fallen nature" characteristic? The same question must be raised about the enmity of Satan against sinners. Satan obviously seems to be against Adam in the garden so how is this characteristic of "fallen nature"? I would argue that it

27. Stamps, "You Asked."

seems that these two things are not characteristic of a fallen nature. While these two are not necessary characteristics of a fallen nature, the enmity of God against sin is a consequence of being fallen. We need to be reconciled to God. Now this project does not have the space to discuss this in further detail, it is necessary for this conversation to move forward that a more detailed examination of this must be had. Scripture tells us that God looks upon Christ in his baptism and says "this is my Son in whom I am well pleased," and yet he turns his back when Christ is hanging on the cross.

Another issue is a lack of clarity on the meaning of nature and person. What is a "nature" and what is a "person"? Crisp sets forth a concrete nature understanding of human nature saying that the human nature is a human body (physical) and human soul (metaphysical) composite.[28] This means that Jesus Christ "consists of God the Son, and a human soul and a human body (i.e. a human nature)."[29] The issue of distinction between person and nature is difficult for there is not one agreed upon understanding of nature and person. Crisp notes that besides the concrete nature view, which states that "Christ's human nature is a concrete particular, perhaps a human body, but, traditionally, a human body and human soul distinct from the Word."[30] On the other side is the abstract nature view that says that Christ's human nature "is a property, or set of properties, necessary and sufficient for being human."[31] Boethius explains it this way. A person is an individual substance of rational nature (this includes understanding). In the incarnation the divine Word assumes a human nature, which is distinct from the Word as its own supposit/person, thus Jesus Christ is one person and two natures.[32] Torrance challenges the Boethean understanding of nature person saying that Boethias' definition is a "philosophical concept derived through logical analysis from Aristotelian and Neoplatonic notions of particular

28. Crisp, "Compositional Christology," 45.

29. Ibid.

30. Crisp, *Divinity and Humanity*, 41.

31. Ibid.

32. Adams, *Christ and Horrors*, 109.

and general substance and rational nature."[33] More exploration of Torrance's understanding of nature and person must be had in order to understand if he is speaking in similar terms that Crisp is. Because of Torrance's understanding of an-hypostasis vs en-hypostasis it appears that he holds to the idea that the nature is a universal property that all human persons share (an-hypostasis) and this universal nature is personalized by each of our individual persons. In the case of Christ he has the universal fallen nature that we all share and he personalizes this universal nature with his divine, pre-existent person. That is, the Second Person of the Trinity (the Son of God) personalizes the universal fallen nature. Torrance would place "mind, will, and body" in the human nature so that it can be said that Christ assumes our original sin and guilt and our "twisted, distorted, bent mind," contained in our actual human nature, and in assuming it "right from the very beginning, our Lord converted it, healed it, and sanctified it in himself."[34] Thus, for Torrance, nature is our mind, will, and body that is in a universal state of fallenness that is personalized (en-hypostatic) by the Divine, Second *Person* of the Trinity.

While Crisp (and Stamps) raises several potential problems with his version of the fallenness view, his arguments fall flat on what seems like a misunderstanding of what those on the fallenness side are actually affirming. Crisp's shortcoming is that he did not examine an actual argument of anyone from the fallenness side rather he created what *he believes* to be the argument (or at least one generalized argument) from the fallenness side. This gives the defenders of the fallenness side reason to be more clear as they move forward in this discussion so as not to be misunderstood in their confession.

---

33. Ho, *A Critical Study*, 142.
34. Torrance, *Atonement*, 440.

Examining the Main Texts of Scripture

At this point this project takes a turn from an examination of other's arguments concerning the fallen or unfallen state of the nature of Christ to examine Scripture and create a potential argument, in light of these critiques and the evidence we have in Scripture, for the fallenness view. This will be done in two parts. The first part will be an examination of these passages in context of the whole chapter and book, and the second part will be an examination of how these texts have been understood by large figures in historical theology such as Calvin and Luther.

Scripture in Context

The first main text that I want to examine is 2 Corinthians 5:21. It says "For our sake he made him to be sin who knew no sin, so that in him we might become the righteousness of God."[35] This verse many people now know because of the popular hit by Chris Tomlin "Jesus Messiah" released in 2008. The song opens with these exact words, "He became sin who knew no sin that we might become his righteousness."[36] This passage has been interpreted to mean that Christ became a "sin offering"[37] or that Christ was "sin's representative."[38] While the idea that Christ was a sin offering, which points back to Old Testament themes, the word used here (*hamartia*), while sometimes used as a reference to "sin offering" in the LXX, "the word *hamartia* does *not* have the meaning 'sin offering' elsewhere in the New Testament, and if Paul intends that meaning here, then he uses the word with two quite different

---

35. All Scripture quotations from the English Standard Version unless otherwise noted.

36. Tomlin, "Jesus Messiah."

37. "From the time of Ambrosiaster and Augustine, interpreters have argued that Paul means that Christ became a 'sin offering'" (Garland, *2 Corinthians*, 5:21). He gets his information from Sabourin, *Sin, Redemption, and Sacrifice*, 185–296.

38. Keener, *The IVP Bible Background Commentary*, 2 Cor 5:21.

meanings in the same sentence."[39] For Paul says in the first line that Christ was "made sin," and in the second he says "who knew no sin." It would seem that if the first use was a "sin offering" the second is not referring to an offering but to *actual* sin. If Paul did mean to say that he became a "sin offering" he would not have said "*made*" sin. He would have been more likely to use "the verb 'presented' or 'offered' rather than 'made.'"[40] It makes more sense, then, to reject the idea that he became merely a "sin offering" and to hold to the idea that "Paul intends to say that Christ was made a sinner."[41] Yet, as we have discussed throughout this project, Christ sinlessness must be maintained. For if Christ "knew sin" his deity would have to be called into question. So while Christ can be said to have been "made sin" it is as important, if not more important, to keep reading, "*who knew no sin*." He was sinner without knowing sin. But why? Paul says so that "we might become the righteousness of God." For the sake of atonement, that's why. While some have said that Christ did this as a representative for us,[42] it seems more appropriate, based on the use of the preposition *hyper* ("instead of another" or "in place of another"[43]), to hold that what Christ did was done in a *substitutionary* fashion. It could be thought of in this way, that "Christ does not become human in order to stand in solidarity with humanity but to stand in its place and to participate in a twofold imputation: he receives the burden of humanity's sin while humanity receives God's righteousness."[44] So what can we know for certain from this passage, what is the bottom line? Simply put, it shows us how our reconciliation was made possible through the person of Jesus Christ. Christ is not merely a

39. Garland, *2 Corinthians*, 5:21.

40. Ibid.

41. Ibid.

42. Hooker argues, "It is as man's *representative*, rather than as his substitute, that Christ suffers, and it is only as one who if fully human that he is able to do anything effective for mankind, by lifting man, as it were, into an obedient relationship with God" (Hooker, "Interchange in Christ," 358). See also Keener, *IVP Bible Background Commentary*.

43. Garland, *2 Corinthians*, 5:21.

44. McLean, *The Cursed Christ*, 112.

representative for us he was a *substitute* for us. "God provided Jesus to stand in for sinful humanity. Even though Jesus was sinless, God deals with him . . ." as a sinner "by letting him die an accursed death. The result of this transaction is that 'we might become the righteousness of God.' We do not simply have righteousness *from* God, we are the righteousness *of* God."[45]

The second text that I want to examine is Romans 8:3. It says, "For God has done what the law, weakened by the flesh, could not do. By sending his own Son in the likeness of sinful flesh and for sin, he condemned sin in the flesh." Paul begins by reminding the audience that the law (this is reference to the Mosaic law) cannot free us from the power of sin. The law is not the medicine that we need to break free from this disease of sin. And so God had the only possible solution to our bondage to sin. He sends Jesus Christ in the incarnation to be our Savior. But what must be noted here is the phrase that Paul uses "in the likeness of sinful flesh." What Paul is emphasizing here is that Jesus Christ was fully participating in "the human condition."[46] This is a very clear articulation against the doetic arguments that Christ only "appeared" to be human. Paul argues that, in fact, Jesus is fully human as we are. But why does he emphasize "sinful" flesh? The word used here, *homoioma*, "probably has the nuance of 'form' rather than 'likeness' or 'copy.' In other words, the word does not suggest superficial or outward similarity, but inward and real participation or 'expression.'"[47] This word gives more of an expression to Christ being exactly like us rather than similar to us. It seems as though Paul wants to affirm that "Christ fully entered into the human condition . . . and as such, exposed himself to the power of sin. On the other hand, he [Paul] must avoid suggesting that Christ so participated in this realm that he became imprisoned 'in the flesh.'"[48] But Paul's main emphasis in this passage is the purpose for Christ coming in the "likeness of sinful flesh." He continues "he condemned sin in the flesh." While

45. Garland, 2 *Corinthians*, 5:21, emphasis mine.
46. Moo, *The Epistle to the Romans*, 8:3.
47. Ibid.
48. Ibid.

there have been many interpretations of what this means,[49] and while these varying interpretations, where they are not contradictory, may be various facets of the same diamond. But the main point is that God, acting as judge, condemned (*katakrinen*) sin in the person of Jesus Christ who was "made sin" for us. As Doug Moo rightly summarizes,

> In doing so, of course, we may say that sin's power was broken, in the sense that Paul pictures sin as a power that holds people in its clutches and brings condemnation to them. In executing the full sentence of condemnation against sin, God effectively removed sin's ability to "dictate terms" for those who are "in Christ" (v. 2). The condemnation that our sins deserve has been poured out on Christ, our sin-bearer; that is why "there is now no condemnation for those who are in Christ Jesus" (v. 1).[50]

All of this is for the sake of atonement and reconciliation. Paul proclaims in Romans 6:5–6 that in our union with Christ our "old self" was crucified and we have been set free from sin because we have died and been raised with Christ.

The next passage I want to examine is Hebrews 2:14. "Since therefore the children share in flesh and blood, he himself likewise partook of the same things, that he might destroy the one who has

49. Florence Morgan Gillman sees a threefold understanding of this text. 1) Within the context of the first four verses of Romans 8 there is no evidence that Paul was interested in differentiating between Christ and all others. Rather the contrasts Paul is addressing in these verses are those of the law and the Spirit of Life versus the law of sin and death and what God accomplished versus what the law was unable to do. 2) Paul did not intend to suggest that only sin dwelling in flesh was affected and that insofar as sin is a power outside of humans it was unaffected. Thus the phrase 'in the flesh' tells "where God's condemnation of sin took place." If this exegesis is correct then "in the flesh" is a reference to Christ. Paul did not have to repeat the word "likeness" since it was already used to denote Christ's full identity with humans. 3) The last reason is that this was probably written under the influence of Philippians 2:7 or the tradition therein known to Paul, where the term, as indicated above, emphasizes Christ's full identity with humans. See Gillman, "Another Look," 597–604. On the other side N. T. Wright seems to think that "sinful flesh" should be considered "sin offering." See Wright, "The Meaning of *Peri Hamartias*," 453–59.

50. Ibid.

the power of death, that is, the devil." The author of Hebrews is making a clear statement that humanity, you and I, both share in what the author calls "flesh and blood." And he notes that while we share in this flesh and blood, our high priest partook in the very same thing. That is Christ "began to share fully the nature of those whom he chose to redeem."[51] While the words used in Hebrews 2 for share (*koinoneo*) and partook (*metecho*) are different words they share the same meaning, "both describe a participation in a shared reality."[52] The difference between the two is in tense of the word (perfect and aorist). The aorist form of *metecho* "indicates that at some point in time and space he took on the fractured humanity that the children by nature 'shared.'"[53]

But again, as with the passages already discussed, the author is very clear to point out that while Christ did partake in our 'flesh and blood,' our fractured humanity, he did so not to remain in it but rather, "that through death he might destroy the one who has the power of death, that is, the devil." It cannot be stressed enough, Christ assuming this fractured humanity is for the sake of atonement. According to the end of this verse, the purpose of his incarnation is twofold: first, that by his death Jesus might break the power of the evil tyrant who held sway over death; and, second that through this same death he might rescue those who had been enslaved."[54] The idea that Christ now partakes in the same humanity that the rest of us share is grounded in the "bond of unity between Christ and his people in the reality of the incarnation." For "in the incarnation the transcendent Son accepted the mode of existence common to all humanity."[55]

51. Bruce, *The Epistle to the Hebrews*, 78.

52. Allen, *Hebrews*, 114.

53. Bruce, *The Epistle to the Hebrews*, 147. In footnote 105 of Bruce's commentary he notes that this word is the "inceptive aorist: The Son 'began to share' in their humanity." While the form of *koinoneo* used of the flesh and blood that the children share "is the emphatic perfect emphasizing the present condition of God's people . . ."

54. O'Brien, *The Letter to the Hebrews*, 114.

55. Lane, *Hebrews* 1–8, 60.

The next passage I want to examine is Hebrews 4:15. "For we do not have a high priest who is unable to sympathize[56] with our weakness, but one who in every respect has been tempted as we are, yet without sin." Crisp believes that one of the main reasons for holding to the fallenness view is so that it can be said that his temptations are real. He ultimately disagrees with the idea that Christ *had* to have a fallen nature in order to be truly tempted as we are as this passage exclaims. But what does this passage actually teach us? Well it is in the context of Jesus being our "great high priest" and the author wants us to understand that though Christ is our great high priest his "transcendence made no difference to his humanity."[57] When the author of Hebrews says that Christ has been "tempted as we are" he is referring to his earthly life where he, according to Hebrews 12:4, "resisted to the point of shedding" his blood. But, as is the case with 2 Corinthians 5:21, Christ is not bound by or enslaved to sin rather the author of Hebrews notes that he was tempted (he was like us) and yet he never committed *actual* sin (he was unlike us). This final phrase "'without sin' indicates that the meaning of the participle must include temptation and not merely testing."[58] Thus, because Christ was able to resist (he did what the first Adam did not do and he did what we cannot do) he wrought for us the victory over sin and death so that (4:16) we can "draw near to the throne of grace, that we may receive mercy in time of need." In the debate of Christ's impeccability/peccability David Allen makes some important notes on this text that apply to that debate. First, the New Testament, as well as Hebrews, emphasizes the sinlessness of Jesus (he knew no sin 2 Cor 5:21, yet without sin Heb 4:15, etc.). Secondly, the debate cannot be settled on this verse alone. Thirdly and finally, "the scriptures also affirm

---

56. "The special nuance of 'sympathize' extends beyond the sharing of feelings. It always includes the element of active help in this context the stress falls on the capacity of the exalted high priest to help those who are helpless. This capacity derives from Christ's full participation in humanity. The heavenly exercise of his office is based upon the accomplishments of his earthly ministry" (ibid., 114).

57. O'Brien, *The Letter to the Hebrews*, 182.

58. Allen, *Hebrews*, 304.

Christ's full identification with fallen humanity with the single exception stated here in v 15: he was without sin."[59]

The final text that I want to quickly look at is John 1:14. "The Word became flesh and made his dwelling among us . . ." This is the most commonly quoted verse on the nature of the incarnation. Carson points out in his commentary on John that it is here that John is completely unambiguous "almost shocking in the expressions he uses *the Word became flesh*."[60] It is here in the "likeness of sinful" flesh, "Into that condition of human weakness the Logos 'pitched his tent.'"[61] Christ does not become incarnate as "an angel or another magnificent creature; He becomes man. Divine majesty abased Himself and became like us poor bag of worms."[62] It is here that "two natures were so united in one person in Christ, that one and the same Christ is true God and *true* man."[63] Seldom do you find someone who wants to affirm that Christ was in a glorified state while he was walking the earth, pre-resurrection, for Christ had to be like us so that he could fix the problem of sin himself. He became the antidote that cured the disease permanently. He is God with us and for us.

A Final Argument

With an understanding of the fallenness view, the critiques of it, and an examination of the major Scripture references used in the debate one other potential argument will be set forth with all of this in mind.

1. The eternal Word, the Second Person of the Trinity, was pre-existent.

2. Mankind fell into sin due to the fall of Adam and Eve in Genesis 1 and 2.

59. Ibid, 306.

60. Carson, *The Gospel According to John*, 126.

61. Beasley-Murray, *John*, 14.

62. Luther, *Luther's Works: Gospel of John*, 102.

63. Calvin, *Calvin's Commentaries*, 17:46.

3. Thus, "the second person of the Trinity elects to take to himself a human nature."[64]

4. This *anhypostatic* nature was *personalized* by the eternal Word of God so that the person of Jesus Christ is that of the Son of God.

5. This nature is that of the same nature that his "children share in flesh and blood" (Heb 2:14).

6. That nature suffers the external consequences of fallenness, that is, *suffering infirmity and temptation, a state of enmity of God against sin, and the enmity of Satan against sinners,* and deals with the ontological corruption of a fallen nature, i.e., corrupt mind and will that are located in the nature.

Because Torrance locates the corrupt mind and will in the nature the two definitions given, while some have argued that there is a change in Torrance's understanding I argue that there is a maturing of his understanding. These are not two distinct definitions but rather two unified definitions. One (without original sin) is focused on Christ's assuming our fallen experience, that is the external consequences of fallenness. The second (with original sin) is distinct in Torrance's theology for he argued in his early theology that Christ did not assume original sin in his later theology he did. However, the two definitions given do not have to be contradictory or distinct. While the former definition focuses on the external consequences, the later gets at the ontological heart of what it means to be fallen and for Torrance (at the very least in his later theology) Christ deals with both the external and internal consequences or characteristics of a fallen nature (human body, soul, will).

7. Christ vicariously takes upon himself this very same human nature.

8. Christ has a fallen human nature (body, soul, and will) and his life was lived in a state *suffering the external pressures of*

64. Crisp, "Did Christ have a Fallen Human Nature?," 280.

infirmity and temptation, and the enmity of Satan against sin-
ners (This can be seen in his temptations), and he takes the
consequences for our fallenness by taking the wrath of God
upon himself and through defeating death provided a new
way of life.

9. Because Jesus' person was that of the Second Person of the
   Trinity he lives in a fallen nature sinlessly.

10. Christ resist's temptation to the point of shedding his blood
    on the cross.

11. The result of Christ's assumption of this fallen nature is the
    "condemnation of sin in the flesh" (Rom 8:3) and our being
    raised to new life (Rom 6).

The purpose of his assuming the same nature that we have,
the "sinful flesh," was never simply so that we can affirm that he
can sympathize with us or to make his temptations "real" but always for the sake of atonement which was the reason that he came.

12. As Christians we now experience this new life (2 Cor 5:17;
    Rom 6:1–4).

Conclusion

This chapter has sought to answer the question *is there a way to re-*
tain what is helpful while avoiding the harmful consequences? I believe that with the arguments laid forth in this chapter that I have
shown that it is possible to hold to a version of the fallenness view
that does make sense and is for the purpose of atonement. While
Crisp and has raised some important critiques of the version the
fallenness view that he set forth, most of which I agree with if one
was to subscribe to *his* version of the fallenness view, I believe that
he would have been better off to critique the argument of someone
who is arguing for the fallenness view rather than create his own
argument. I believe that it is possible to hold this version of the
fallenness view that does not put orthodoxy in jeopardy by saying that Christ was not impeccable or that Christ was corrupt or

loathsome in the sight of God. For if these things are the case, then Crisp is right to raise concern for it places Christ's ability to be our Savior in jeopardy and thus places us in jeopardy and leaves us needing a Savior

This whole project is based on the question *while remaining orthodox, can it be said that Christ assumed a fallen human nature in the incarnation?* I believe that understood properly it can be said that he assumed a fallen human nature in the incarnation. But I conclude with this thought, while I believe that it is important that we study and understand this question it is in no way a debate that should split the church or even cause discord among people in Christ's church for our very union with Christ not only reconciles us to God but in reconciling us to God we are reconciled to each other. I, also, have not ended the debate. I have merely addressed some of the possible concerns that Crisp set forth concerning one other potential understanding of the fallenness view. Here I have set forth one other possible option of understanding the fallenness view with the help of T. F. Torrance and an examination of Scripture.

A lot of claims have been made throughout these chapters, some things that must be confessed, others that are simply plausible options to this debate. But since theologians minister the eschatological reality of "the truth of being-in-Christ"[65] we now conclude with several things, based on the evidence, which we can confess as reality of being in Christ without stepping into much plausible speculation.

1. Christ is sinless. The testimony of Scripture is very clear that Christ remained sinless throughout his entire life. He lived his life in complete obedience to his Father's will. This obedience led him to the cross where he gave his life for us and was raised to new life so that we may have new life. Any form of the fallenness view that contradicts this or puts this in jeopardy should be called unorthodox.[66]

---

65. Vanhoozer, *The Pastor as Public Theologian*, 111.

66. In his "active and passive obedience we are to think of Christ as dealing

2. Christ truly was tempted as we are and yet he resisted this temptation in his obedience to the Father.

3. Christ took the full punishment for our sin in such a way that the Father turned his back. Gerritt Scott Dawson puts it so well

> What man cannot do for himself, God has done for him, in the Man on the Cross. "My God, My God, why has though forsaken me." Theological inquiry cannot hurry past that terrible cry of God-forsakenness of the Man on the Cross; for it is there that we are carried to the extreme edges of our existence, to the very brink of the abysmal chasm that separates us from God. It is there that we see the end of all our theologizing, in sheer God-forsakenness, in the desolate waste where God is hidden from us by our sin and self-will and self-inflicted blindness and where, as it were, God has "died out on us" and is nowhere to be found by man. He bent our human nature in himself back to the obedience of the Father.[67]

4. Christ truly and really atoned for our sins as the *spotless* Lamb of God who takes away the sins of the world.

Kelly Kapic has helpfully pointed out several ways in which both sides of this debate can be united.

1. Both fallen and unfallen adherents oppose those who have treated Mary simply as a channel, affirming rather that the Son is able from mary to assume a complete human nature: including a reasonable soul . . . and physical body.

---

with our *actual* sins through the atoning exchange of His life and death and resurrection, but we cannot do that without also thinking of His incarnational union of our human nature with His divine nature as dealing with our original sin, or as sanctifying our fallen human nature *through* bringing it into healing and sanctifying union with His holy divine nature" (Torrance *The School of Faith*, 1xxxvi).

67. Dawson, *An Introduction to Torrance Theology*, 73.

2. Both positions affirm that the incarnate Son of God entered not a pre-fallen paradise, but a sin ravaged world as the true son of fallen Mary; thus the Son assumed our common infirmities and weaknesses . . . As such, Jesus is never outside a relationship to a sinful and chaotic world.

3. Both positions affirm the Holy Spirit's involvement in allowing Jesus Christ to be "without sin." The unfallen position claims that because of the Spirit's sanctifying work at conception it is impossible to speak iof a time when the human nature was fallen, although the spirit's activity does not end at conception but remains essential for the incarnate Lord to continue in obedience. The fallen position emphasizes the Spirit's role in keeping the *person* of Christ free from sin, thgouh the human nature is itself "sinful flesh."

4. Both sides believe that the temptations of Jesus were not empty drama but agonizing experiences, allowing him to be a sympathetic high priest.

5. In contemporary theological discourse, fundamental to being human is relationship to others and to God. If we simply say that Jesus experiences the painful realities of human relationships in a sin infected world, then both sides can agree.[68]

In conclusion, based on the arguments set forth in this project it appears is possible to remain orthodox and hold to the fallenness view, this project is has sought to be helpful in clarifying exactly what is mean when we say that Christ assumed a fallen human nature and to help clear up some, what I believe to be, misconceptions of the fallenness view that has placed it in the unorthodox category. So I hope that from here we can move forward with more clarity so that we can have genuine dialogue with each other as we work together to understand God more fully.

68. Kapic, "The Son's Assmption," 164–65.

Chapter 5

Christ and the Spirit

"For since he came to share our human nature and
we are united to him through the Spirit which he gives
us, it is through the power of the same Spirit that we
participate in prokope, and so rise through the Son
to true knowledge of, and communion with God the
Father."[1]

T. F. TORRANCE

Introduction

IN 2009, THEN PASTOR Francis Chan released a book called
Forgotten God: Reversing Our Tragic Neglect of the Holy Spirit. In
this book, Chan argues, "the Holy Spirit is tragically neglected and,
for all practical purposes, forgotten."[2] He continues that while no
proclaiming evangelical would deny the actual existence of the
Spirit, he bets that there are millions of regular church attenders
who cannot say with confidence that they have *experienced* the
Spirit's presence or activity in their lives and, tragically, many do
not think that it is possible to experience the Spirit. It seems many
have even fallen prey to the ideology that says "I have Jesus! Why

---

1. Torrance, *Theology in Reconstruction*, 246.
2. Chan, *Forgotten God*, 15.

do I need the Spirit?"[3] If we are struggling with understanding why *we* need the Spirit it is no wonder that to ask the question "why does *Jesus* need the Spirit" seems ludicrous! But I believe that this is a question that must be asked especially in light of the conversation of this book. This chapter, thus, seeks to briefly address how Spirit Christology could help us answer the meta question of this book, *is it possible, while remaining orthodox, to argue that Christ assumed a fallen human nature?*

What is Spirit Christology?

To ask the question, "why does Jesus need the Spirit" is to partake in what systematic theologians call *Spirit Christology*. It is not simple to define exactly what "Spirit Christology" is. There are several different ways in which to understand what this is. One way to understand it is through the lens of Anglican theologian Geofrey Lampe. Lampe says that "The use of this concept [Spirit Christology] enables us to say that God indwelt and motivated the human spirit of Jesus in such a way that in him, uniquely, the relationship for which man is intended by his Creator was fully realized."[4] Another way of understanding it is that the Holy Spirit's work is to sustain the human nature of Christ during his private and public ministry beginning at the moment of incarnation. This view is put forth by Roman Catholic theologian Ralph Del Colle in his book *Christ and the Spirit: Spirit Christology in Trinitarian Perspective* from Oxford University Press. Probably, the most famous or well-known instance of Spirit Christology is from Reformed theologian John Owen. Owens has argued that the "only singular immediate act of the person of the Son on the human nature was the assumption of it into subsistence with himself."[5] In other words, "The Holy Ghost, as we have proved before, is the immediate, peculiar, efficient cause of all external divine operations: for God worketh by

3. This is the title of Chan's second chapter.

4. Lampe, *God as Spirit*, 11.

5. Owen, *Works*, 160.

his Spirit, or in him immediately applies the power and efficacy of the divine excellencies unto their operation; whence the same work is equally the work of each person."[6]

Now, my goal is not to give an exposition of history of the development of Spirit Christology, but rather to emphasize the need for an orthodox Spirit Christology as we attempt to see how this Spirit Christology could help us in the fallen nature debate. As with any doctrine or method of theology, it comes with its critics. One of the biggest critiques specifically against Torrance is Kevin Chiarot. His critiques have already been talked about in earlier chapters, but, as Myk Habets has helpfully pointed out, at the heart of his critique

> is an underlying issue—namely, that in Chiarot's reading of Torrance, the idea of a universal ontological solidarity with all humanity is a fiction, and that even if such a thing were possible, it could not be rendered intelligible, especially if such humanity is fallen, thus Torrance's theology at this point [7]

gives us reason to question the *non assumptus*. Chiarot's solution to this apparent problem is to speak in forensic rather than ontological terms as Torrance does. It seems unfair to critique Torrance with a different method than he would have used himself. If forensic theology is not a fair way to make sense of Torrance's theology then we must try a different way. Dr. Habets suggests "Torrance scholarship must move towards illustrating something like the Spirit Christology implicit in Torrance's work . . ."[8] What follows is a brief attempt to examine Torrance's theology concerning the Spirit's relationship with the person of Christ.

6. Ibid, 162.

7. Habets, "The Fallen Humanity of Christ," 34.

8. Ibid, 35.

Spirit Christology and the Humanity of Christ

Torrance is known for his christocentric theology but less focus and time has been given to understanding his pneumatology. He argues that Christ, in our fallen flesh, "condemned sin in it; he overcame its temptations, resisted its downward drag in alienation from God, and converted it back in himself to obedience toward God, thus sanctifying it . . ."[9] Every time that I have taught on this topic the question is always asked, "Ok, but *how* does he sanctify it?" I believe Torrance answers this question well using Luke 2:52 to respond. The verse begins by stating that "Jesus grew in wisdom and stature . . ." Torrance translates "grew" saying that Jesus "beat his way forward"[10] taking a human nature that is defined by its bent toward itself and unbending it back toward God. But, for Torrance, this is not something done strictly by the Second Person of the Trinity. Jesus' life is at every turn an act of the Logos and the Spirit from his virginal conception (conceived by the Holy Spirit as the Apostles' creed claims), baptism in the Jordan (The Holy Spirit descends on him like a dove), his ministry, etc. It is critical that when we examine the life of Christ we look at the role of the Spirit in the life of Christ as well. For Torrance, the baptism of Jesus is significant in this examination for it is at his baptism that Jesus lived "not simply as Son of God but as Son of God become man, as Son of Man, that is to live it out from beginning to end within the limitations of our creaturely humanity, and within the limitations of our humanity in the house of bondage."[11]

It seems easy to argue that Jesus lived a perfect life simply out of his divine person but the Gospel narratives clearly show Jesus' reliance on the Spirit throughout his life. When Jesus is lead into the wilderness and is tempted by Satan, the text points out that he is lead by the Spirit during this time. Everything that Jesus did he did out of dependence on the Spirit and not simply out of his divine nature. Torrance says

9. Torrance, *Incarnation*, 205.

10. Ibid, 64 and 106.

11. Ibid, 123.

> He was never without the Spirit for as the eternal Son he
> remained in the unity of the Spirit and of the Father, but
> as Incarnate Son on earth he was given the Spirit without
> measure and consecrated in his human nature for his
> mission as the vicarious Servant. He came through the
> temptations in the wilderness clothes with the power of
> the Spirit and went forth to bring in the Kingdom of God
> by meeting and defeating the powers of darkness en-
> trenched in human flesh. He struggled and prayed in the
> Spirit with unspeakable cries of agony, and bore in his
> Spirit the full burden of human evil and woe. Through
> the eternal Spirit he offered himself without spot to the
> Father in sacrifice for sin; according to the Spirit of holi-
> ness he was raised from the dead, and ascended to the
> right hand of the Father to receive all power in heaven
> and earth. There he attained the ground from which he
> could pour out the Spirit of God upon all flesh.[12]

The role of the Spirit is critical because it is "through the power of
the same Spirit that we participate in prokope, and so rise through
the Son to true knowledge of, and communion with God the
Father."[13] Because we experience the healing of our fallen humanity through the Spirit and through the Spirit's uniting us to Christ
it can be said that there is "a vicarious activity of the Spirit which
matches the vicarious work of the Son."[14]

Some have raised criticism of this understanding of Spirit
Christology for several reasons. Since Oliver Crisp has been my
main opponent in this writing I will work with his critique. He argues that Spirit Christology leaves no "metaphysical room for the
interposition of another divine person between the intentions of
God the Son (i.e. his agency) and the intentional actions brought
about in his human nature."[15] In other words, Spirit Christology
actual drives a wedge between the Logos (Second Person of the
Trinity) and the human nature that he assumes. Crisp thinks that

12. Torrance, *Theology in Reconstruction*, 246.

13. Ibid, 39.

14. Habets, "The Fallen Humanity of Christ," 37.

15. Crisp, *Revisioning Christology*, 92.

to Spirit Christology substitutes the acting subject of the Christ's person with the Spirit which is a denial of the very incarnation of the Son. Habets helpfully summarizes his critique saying, "Crisp's central critique is that a Spirit Christology is untenable on the grounds that once the Son has assumed human nature he steps back and lets the Holy Spirit act in all future works."[16] Thus, the Logos has no active participation in his obedience. If this is indeed where Spirit Christology leads, then I agree with Crisp that this is problematic. So let us see if there is a way that we can move forward from this critique.

It would seem that Crisp's critique, while taking into account the hypostatic union, fails to take into account the *perichoresis*. Habets defines perichoresis as "in the one simple being of the triune God all three persons mutually indwell the other such that the threeness of the persons is the oneness of the essences."[17] In other words, the Trinity is three persons in one *UNDIVIDED* substance. The three persons are so undivided in nature that even in their mission they are undivided. Thus we could say that even though the Son is the main character in the incarnation it is never without the participation of the Father and the Son. Based on these claims Habets argues that this makes "clear that the divine agency in the incarnation is that of the Son and the Spirit, in their respective ways. The Son is the willing subject . . . [and] the Spirit is the active *paracletos*, no less personal or involved."[18] Crisp is afraid that Spirit Christology gives active agency to the Spirit to the exclusion of the Son.[19] So if Torrance is advocating that Christ takes a backseat to the Spirit then there are problems with Spirit Christology. However, Habets argues that this is not what Torrance is doing, "rather, [he is] providing an account of the incarnation in which there is dual agency at work, that of the Son and the Spirit, and both in personal and appropriate ways."[20] We have to maintain, in

16. Habets, "The Fallen Nature of Christ," 39.

17. Ibid, 39.

18. Ibid, 40.

19. Crisp, *Revisioning Christology*, 107.

20. Habets, "The Fallen Humanity of Christ," 41.

line with Chalcedonian Christology, that Christ's human nature is exactly like other human beings for he completely shares in our human nature. But Christ is unlike us because he has a different hypostasis or person which is what makes him unique. Ian MacFarland argues that

> an emphasis on the role of the Spirit enables this Chalcedonian insight to be developed more consistently than has often been the case by allowing Christ's humanity to be construed holistically: as a complete nature that, although at every point moved and shaped by the Spirit, remains in both being and act utterly distinct from divinity.[21]

Habets argues that he believes this is what Torrance is arguing for as long "as 'distinct' means that and not 'independent' or 'separate.'"[22] The question I now ask is is Habets assessment of Torrance's argument accurate? Does Torrance understand the role of the Spirit in Christ's life to be working with the Logos or working instead of the Logos? I now turn to examine Torrance's understanding of the role of the Spirit in the life of Christ.

TORRANCE, THE SPIRIT, AND CHRIST

Torrance is known for his deeply christological writings and meaningful theological expositions of the life of Christ and he is well known for the right reasons. However, it would seem that it is less well known how Torrance understands the Spirit to work in the life of Christ. This section seeks to understand how Torrance understands the Spirit to operate in the life of Christ. As Elmer Coyler helpfully points out, "We have to view Jesus' entire life, ministry, death, and resurrection in Pneumatological terms as well."[23]

---

21. MacFarland, "Spirit and Incarnation," 144.
22. Habets, "The Fallen Humanity of Christ," 42.
23. Coyler, "Thomas F. Torrance," 162.

As we have already seen throughout this work, Torrance believes that our union with God comes through our human nature united to the human nature of the incarnate Christ, then Christ's human nature *had* to be (vicariously) fallen in order to redeem our fallen natures. To speak any other way would be to fall into what Torrance called the "Latin Heresy." There is an ontological nature to our problem, namely sin. Thus, there must be an ontological nature to our solution, namely Jesus Christ and his salvation. Torrance explains this ontological exchange in this way

> He was very man, our Brother. In him the Holy Son of God was grafted on to the stock of our fallen human existence, and in him our mortal and corrupt human nature was assumed into union with the Holy Son of God, so that in Jesus, in his birth and sinless life, in his death and resurrection, there took place a holy and aweful judgment on our flesh of sin, and an atoning sanctification of our unholy human existence. *It was through such atonement that God in all his Godness and holiness came to dwell in the midst of mortal, sinful man.*[24]

He continues by saying, "this is the way that the divine love has taken to redeem man, by making him share in the holy power in which God lives his own divine life."[25] Torrance is clearly referencing the Spirit here since the Spirit is the way in which God dwells with man. However, this is not a clear reference to how the Spirit actual operates within this plan of atonement. This reference seems more a side note pointing out that the Spirit simply applies to us what Christ did for us in his life, death, and resurrection.

Torrance often quotes the patristic axiom "the unassumed is the unhealed," which was used by theologians like Gregory of Nazianzen and Tertullian to argue against apollinarianism that said that Jesus did not have a human mind but a divine mind. This axiom was used to defend the full humanity of Jesus including a human mind. As Dr. Habets points out, Apollinaris rejected the idea that Jesus had a human mind because that was thought to be

24. Torrance, *Theology in Reconciliation*, 241.

25. Ibid.

the seat of sin.[26] Thus, in rejecting apollinarianism, Torrance actually argues that Christ assumed a human will that is subject to the fall. But in assuming it, Christ redeems the fallen mind.[27] If Christ assumed a human body without a human will, then he is not fully human and he would not experience our human experiences such as growth, pain, anguish, distress, etc. Torrance clearly argues that Christ had to assume a human will and "it is indeed precisely in this area that the essential work of redemption took place, where the inward and outward man are one and inseparable, and where Christ's redeeming work was no less a work of his soul than a work of his body."[28] For Torrance, redemption has to be a whole redemption or humanity still needs a savior. He says so well,

> In allowing no room for the mental and moral life of Jesus as man an in denying to him the authentic human agency in his saving work, it left no place for the vicarious role of the human soul and mind and will of Jesus in the reconciling exchange of like for like in the redemption of man. And by destroying his representative capacity, it had no place for his priesthood or human mediation in our worship of the Father, and by the same token it took away the ground for any worship of God with our human minds. A mutilated humanity in Christ could not but result in a mutilated Christian worship of God.[29]

In regards to the constitution of the whole being of Christ we must say that he was one person (the Logos) inseparably joining together two natures, human and divine. Because his person is the Logos, the eternal Son of God, he is without sin and thus not guilty. However, he can vicariously assume a fallen human nature and remain guiltless and therefore, not at enmity with God. It is in this state that Torrance says,

> there was no sin in him which allowed [death] to subject him to corruption. Death had nothing in him, for he had

26. Habets, "The Fallen Humanity of Christ," 26.

27. Torrance leans on Karl Barth for this. Torrance, *Karl Barth*, 104, 202–5.

28. Torrance, *Theology in Reconciliation*, 149.

29. Ibid., 150.

already passed through its clutches by the perfection of his holiness. He triumphed over the grave through sheer sinlessness. The resurrection is thus the resurrection of the union forged between man and God in Jesus out of damned and lost condition of men into which Christ entered in order to share their lot and redeem them from doom.[30]

Torrance's writings focus more directly on the "person" vs. "nature" argument when it comes to the fallen nature question, but his theology is not absent of the Spirit. He argues that there is nothing in the life of Christ that happens apart from the Spirit (for instance his conception, baptism, spirit anointed ministry, etc.). He argues that,

> Jesus Christ was born of the virgin Mary into our human nature through the power of the Spirit; at his baptism the Holy Spirit descended upon him and anointed him as the Christ. He was never without the Spirit for as the eternal Son he ever remained in the unity of the Spirit and of the Father, but as Incarnate Son on earth he was given the Spirit without measure and consecrated in his human nature for his mission as the vicarious Servant. He came through the temptations in the wilderness clothed with the power of the Spirit and went forth to bring in the Kingdom of God by meeting and defeating the powers of darkness entrenched in human flesh. He struggled and prayed in the Spirit with unspeakable cries of agony, and bore in his Spirit the full burden of human evil and woe. Through the eternal Spirit he offered himself without spot to the Father in sacrifice for sin; according to the Spirit of Holiness he was raised from the dead, and ascended to the right hand of the Father to receive all power in heaven and earth. There he attained the ground from which he could pour out the Spirit of God upon all flesh.[31]

---

30. Torrance, *Space, Time, and Resurrection*, 53–54.

31. Torrance, *Theology in Reconstruction*, 246.

For Torrance, then, the active obedience of Jesus Christ through the power of the Spirit had a huge part to play in our whole redemption.

CONCLUSION

I do not believe that Torrance was clear enough about the role of the Holy Spirit in the life of Christ to establish what Torrance's thoughts on Spirit Christology are *in totum*. It is clear that the Spirit is critical to Torrance's Christology but it seems to be assumed that the Spirit played a large role in the obedience of Christ in flesh. Scholars such as Oliver Crisp have raised objections to this idea, though, arguing, "it introduces a theologically damaging cleavage between God the Son and his human nature."[32] He believes that to say that the Spirit played this role in Christ's life then you must deny that Christ is the subject of the incarnation. If this is what Torrance argues then Crisp has ground to stand on but it is clear from Torrance's writings that this is not what he intends to do. I agree with Dr. Habets that "Contemporary proposals for Spirit Christology which are conducive to Torrance's theology affirm that in the one simple being of the triune God all three persons mutually indwell the other such that the threeness of the persons is the oneness of the essence."[33] Based on the doctrine of the perichoresis we can say that "while the Son is the subject of the incarnation, this is not without the Father and the Son."[34]

If we are to move forward in the conversation concerning Christ's assumption of a fallen human nature and we wish to remain orthodox, then I would argue that we need to move into the world of Spirit Christology as Dr. Habets argues. If we can come to an understanding of the role of the Spirit in the life of Christ then we may be able to make more sense of Christ assuming a fallen nature. I believe, though, that Torrance is not as clear on this topic

32. Crisp, *Revisioning Christology*, 92.

33. Habets, "The Fallen Humanity of Christ," 39

34. Ibid.

as is necessary and thus, we must establish a Spirit Christology and then reapproach Torrance's Christology. This will help us come to a fuller understanding of this debate and Torrance's theology. As Dr. Habets argues, "Such a clarification of Torrance's theology, one in which the Holy Spirit is more prominent, offers a dogmatic and pastoral advantage over most text-book approaches to theology; and also a way in which to address the critique of Torrance's doctrine of the *non assumptus* has attracted."[35]

35. Ibid, 44.

Appendix

Discovering Torrance

"Now in the twenty-first century the impact of his work is still being felt as PhDs are completed on his work, monographs roll off the presses detailing and critiquing aspects of his theology, and societies and even entire denominations are established to disseminate central features of his thought."

PAUL MOLNAR

WHEN YOU ATTEMPT TO study someone like Torrance, and you want to read what he wrote yourself, the task can be daunting with the amount of material written by him. In this appendix I have compiled a list of the books written by Torrance that are accessible for your research and edification. If you are more interested in comprehensive bibliographies of all of Torrance's published work I am currently aware of three bibliographies. All of Torrance's writings, published and unpublished, can be found in the Torrance Archives at Princeton Seminary.

Gray, Bryan. "Bibliography of the Published Writings of Thomas F. Torrance (1941-1975)." In *Creation, Christ and Culture: Studies in Honour of T. F. Torrance*, edited by R. W. A. McKinney, 307–21. Edinburgh: T. & T. Clark, 1976.

Torrance, Iain. "A Bibliography of the Writings of Thomas F. Torrance, 1941–1989." *Scottish Journal of Theology* 43 (1990) 225–62.

McGrath, Alister. "A Complete Bibliography of the Writings of Thomas F. Torrance 1941–." In *T. F. Torrance: An Intellectual Biography*, edited by Alister McGrath, 249–96. Edinburgh: T. & T. Clark, 1999.

Books

Thomas F. Torrance. *The Apocalypse Today*. Grand Rapids: Eerdmans, 1959.

———. *Atonement: The Person and Work of Christ*. Downers Grove, IL: IVP Academic, 2014.

———. *Calvin's Doctrine of Man*. Eugene, OR: Wipf & Stock, 1997.

———. *The Christian Doctrine of God: One Being Three Persons*. 2nd ed. Edinburgh: T. & T. Clark, 2016.

———. *The Christian Frame of Mind*. Eugene, OR: Wipf & Stock, 2015.

———. *Christian Theology and Scientific Culture*. Eugene, OR: Wipf & Stock, 1998.

———. *Conflict and Agreement in the Church*. Vol. 1, *Order and Disorder*. Eugene, OR: Wipf & Stock, 1996.

———. *Conflict and Agreement in the Church*. Vol. 2, *The Ministry and the Sacraments of the Gospel*. London: Lutterworth, 1959.

———. *Divine and Contingent Order*. Oxford Scholarly Classics. Oxford: Oxford University Press, 2000.

———. *Divine Meaning: Studies in Patristic Hermeneutics*. Edinburgh: T. & T. Clark, 1995.

———. *The Doctrine of Grace in the Apostolic Fathers*. Eugene, OR: Wipf & Stock, 1996.

———. *The Doctrine of Jesus Christ: The Auburn Lectures 1938–1939*. Eugene, OR: Wipf & Stock, 2001.

———. *God and Rationality*. Oxford Scholarly Classics. Oxford: Oxford University Press, 2000.

———. *Gospel, Church, and Ministry*. Edited by Jock Stein. Eugene, OR: Wipf & Stock, 2012.

———. *Ground and Grammar of Theology: Consonance Between Theology and Science*. Edinburgh: T. & T. Clark, 2005.

———. *The Hermeneutics of John Calvin: Monograph Supplements to the Scottish Journal of Theology*. Edinburgh: Scottish Academic Press, 1987.

———. *Incarnation: The Person and Life of Christ*. Downers Grove, IL: IVP Academic, 2015.

———. *Juridicial Law and Physical Law: Toward a Realist Foundation for Human Law*. Eugene, OR: Wipf & Stock, 1997.

———. *Karl Barth: An Introduction to His Early Theology, 1910–1931*. London: SCM, 1962.

———. *Karl Barth: Biblical and Evangelical Theologian*. Edinburgh: T. & T. Clark, 2001.

———. *Kingdom and the Church*. Eugene, OR: Wipf & Stock, 1996.

————. *The Mediation of Christ*. Rev. ed. Colorado Springs: Helmers & Howard, 1992.

————. *Preaching Christ Today: The Gospel and Scientific Thinking*. Grand Rapids: Eerdmans, 1994.

————. *Reality and Evangelical Theology: The Realism of Christian Revelation*. Eugene, OR: Wipf & Stock, 2003.

————. *Reality and Scientific Theology*. Eugene, OR: Wipf & Stock, 2001.

————. *Royal Priesthood*. Edinburgh: T. & T. Clark, 2000.

————. *The School of Faith: Catechisms of the Reformed Church*. Eugene, OR: Wipf & Stock, 1996.

————. *Scottish Theology: From John Knox to John McLeod Campbell*. Edinburgh: T. & T. Clark, 2000.

————. *Space, Time and Incarnation*. Edinburgh: T. & T. Clark, 2005.

————. *Space, Time and Resurrection*. Edinburgh: T. & T. Clark, 2000.

————. *Theological and Natural Science*. Eugene, OR: Wipf & Stock, 2002.

————. *Theological Science*. Edinburgh: T. & T. Clark, 2000.

————. *Theology in Reconciliation*. Eugene, OR: Wipf & Stock, 1996.

————. *Theology in Reconstruction*. Eugene, OR: Wipf & Stock, 1996.

————. *Transformation and Convergence in the Frame of Knowledge: Explorations in the Interrelations of Scientific and Theological Enterprise*. Eugene, OR: Wipf & Stock, 1998.

————. *The Trinitarian Faith*. 2nd ed. Edinburgh: T. & T. Clark, 2016.

————. *Trinitarian Perspectives: Toward Doctrinal Agreement*. Edinburgh: T. & T. Clark, 1994.

————. *When Christ Comes and Comes Again*. Eugene, OR: Wipf & Stock, 1996.

Bibliography

Adams, Marilyn McCord. *Christ and Horrors: The Coherence of Christology.* Cambridge: Cambridge University Press, 2006.

Allen, David. *Hebrews: An Exegetical and Theological Exposition of the Holy Scriptures.* New American Commentary. Nashville: B&H Academic, 2010.

Augustine. *The Trinity.* Translated by Edmund Hill. New York: New City, 1991.

Barth, Karl. *Church Dogmatics.* Edited by G. W. Bromiley and T. F. Torrance. Edinburgh: T. & T. Clark, 1957–1981.

———. *Table Talk.* Edited by John D. Godsey. Richmond, VA: John Knox, 1963.

Beasley-Murray, George R. *John.* Word Biblical Commentary. Dallas: Word, 2002.

Berkhof, Louis. *Systematic Theology.* Edinburgh: Banner of Truth, 1939.

Bruce, F. F. *The Epistle to the Hebrews.* New International Commentary on the New Testament. Grand Rapids: Eerdmans, 1997.

Brunner, Emil. *The Mediator.* Translated by Olive Wyon. Philadelphia: Westminster, 1947.

Burrell, David B. "Divine and Contingent Order." *Theology Today* 39/3 (October 1982) 325–27.

Calvin, John. *Calvin's Commentaries.* 46 vols. Grand Rapids: Baker, 2009.

Carson, D. A. *The Gospel according to John.* Pillar New Testament Commentary. Grand Rapids: Eerdmans, 1991.

Cass, Peter. *Christ Condemned Sin in the Flesh: Thomas F. Torrance's Doctrine of Soteriology and Its Ecumenical Significance.* Saarbrücken, Ger.: Müller, 2009.

Chan, Francis. *Forgotten God: Reversing Our Tragic Neglect of the Holy Spirit.* Colorado Springs: David Cook, 2009.

Chiarot, Kevin. *The Unassumed Is the Unhealed: The Humanity of Christ in the Christology of T. F. Torrance.* Eugene, OR: Pickwick, 2013.

Cole, Graham. *The God Who Became Human: A Biblical Theology of Incarnation.* Downers Grove, IL: IVP Academic, 2013.

Colyer, Elmer M. *How To Read T. F. Torrance: Understanding His Trinitarian and Scientific Theology.* Eugene, OR: Wipf & Stock, 2007.

———. "Thomas F. Torrance on the Holy Spirit." *Word and World* 23/2 (2003) 160–67.

Crisp, Oliver D. "Compositional Christology Without Nestorianism." In *The Metaphysics of the Incarnation*, edited by Jonathan Hill and Anna Marmodoro, 45–66. Oxford: Oxford University Press, 2011.

———. "Did Christ Have a Fallen Human Nature?" *International Journal of Systematic Theology* 6/3 (July 2004) 270–88.

———. *Divinity and Humanity*. Cambridge: Cambridge University Press, 2007.

———. *God Incarnate: Explorations in Christology*. Edinburgh: T. & T. Clark, 2009.

———. "Original Sin and Atonement." In *Oxford Handbook of Philosophical Theology*, edited by Thomas P. Flint and Michael C. Rea, 430–51. Oxford: Oxford University Press, 2011.

———. *Revisioning Christology: Theology in the Reformed Tradition*. Farnham: Ashgate, 2011.

Deddo, Gary. "The Realist and Onto-Relational Frame of T. F. Torrance's Incarnational and Trinitarian Theology." *Theology in Scotland* 16 (2009) 105–33.

Dawson, Gerrit Scott. *An Introduction to Torrance Theology: Discovering the Incarnate Saviour*. Edinburgh: T. & T. Clark, 2007.

Frankfurt, Harry G. *The Importance of What We Care About*. Cambridge: Cambridge University Press, 1998.

Garland, David. *2 Corinthians*. New American Commentary. Nashville: Broadman & Holman, 1999.

Gillman, Florence Morgan. "Another Look At Romans 8:3: 'In The Likeness Of Sinful Flesh.'" *Catholic Biblical Quarterly* 49/4 (1987) 597–604.

Gregory, of Nazianzus. "To Cledonius the Priest Against Apollinarius." In *Cyril of Jerusalem, Gregory Nazianzen*, edited by Phillip Schaff, 7:439–44. Nicene and Post-Nicene Fathers, series 2. Grand Rapids: Eerdmans, 2005. http://www.ccel.org/ccel/schaff/npnf207.iv.ii.iii.html.

Gross, Jules. *Divination of the Christian according to the Greek Fathers*. Anaheim: Living Stream Ministry, 2003.

Habets, Myk. *The Annointed Son: A Trinitarian Spirit Christology*. Eugene, OR: Wipf & Stock, 2010.

———. "The Fallen Humanity of Christ: A Pneumatlogical Clarification of the Theology of Thomas F. Torrance." *Participatio* 5 (2015) 18–44.

———. *The Spirit of Truth: Reading Scripture and Constructing Theology with the Holy Spirit*. Eugene, OR: Pickwick, 2015.

———. "'Suffer the little children to come to me, for theirs is the kingdom of heaven.': Infant Salvation and the Destiny of the Severely Mentally Disabled." In *Evangelical Calvinism: Essays Resourcing the Continuing Reformation of the Church*, edited by Myk Habets and Robert Grow, 287–328. Eugene, OR: Pickwick, 2012.

Heppe, Heinrich. *Reformed Dogmatics*. Eugene, OR: Wipf & Stock, 2008.

Hill, Jonathan, and Anna Marmodoro, eds. *The Metaphysics of the Incarnation*. Oxford: Oxford University Press, 2011.

Ho, Man Kei. *A Critical Study on T. F. Torrance's Theology of Incarnation*. Bern: Wissenschaften, 2008.

Hodge, Charles. *Systematic Theology*. Vol. 2. Edinburgh: Thomas Nelson, 1874.

Hooker, M. D. "Interchange in Christ." *Journal of Theological Studies* 22 (1971) 349–61.

Jones, Paul D. *The Humanity of Christ: Christology in Karl Barth's Church Dogmatics*. New York: T. & T. Clark, 2008.

Kang, Phee Seng. "The Concept of the Vicarious Humanity of Christ in the Theology of Thomas Forsyth Torrance." PhD diss., University of Aberdeen, 1983.

Kapic, Kelly M. "The Son's Assumption of a Human Nature: A Call for Clarity." *International Journal of Systematic Theology* 3/2 (July 2001) 154–66.

Keener, Craig. *The IVP Bible Background Commentary: New Testament*. Downers Grove, IL: InterVarsity, 1993.

Lampe, Geofrey. *God as Spirit: The Baptism Lectures 1976*. Oxford: Oxford University Press, 1977.

Lane, William. *Hebrews 1-8*. Word Biblical Commentary. Westchester: Thomas Nelson, 1991.

Luther, Martin. *Bondage of the Will*. Edited by J. I Packer and O. R. Johnston. Grand Rapids: Baker Academic, 2012.

———. *Luther's Works*. Edited by Jaroslav Pelikan. St. Louis: Concordia, 1958.

Mackintosh, Hugh Ross. *The Doctrine of the Person of Jesus Christ*. Edinburgh: T. & T. Clark, 1945.

———. *The Chrisian Experience of Forgiveness*. London: Nisbet, 1938.

Macleod, Donald. "Christology." In *Dictionary of Scottish Church History and Theology*, edited by Nigel M. de S. Cameron et al., 175. Edinburgh: T. & T. Clark, 1993.

———. "Did Christ Have a Fallen Human Nature?" *The Monthly Record of the Free Church of Scotland* (March 1984) 51–53.

———. *Jesus is Lord: Christology Yesterday and Today*. Fearn, UK: Mentor, 2000.

———. *The Person of Christ*. Leicester: InterVarsity, 1998.

McGrath, Alister E. *T. F. Torrance: An Intellectual Biography*. Edinburgh: T. & T. Clark, 1999.

McFarland, Ian A. "Fallen or Unfallen? Christ's Human Nature and the Ontology of Human Sinfulness." *International Journal of Systematic Theology* 10/4 (October 2008) 399–415.

———. "Willing Is Not Choosing: Some Anthropological Implications of Dyothelite Christology." *International Journal of Systematic Theology* 9/1 (2007) 3–23.

McLean, B. H. *The Cursed Christ: Mediterranean Expulsion Rituals and Pauline Soteriology*. Sheffield: Sheffield Academic Press, 1996.

Molnar, Paul D. *Thomas F. Torrance: Theologian of the Trinity*. Great Theologians. Farnham: Ashgate, 2009.

Moo, Doug. *The Epistle to the Romans.* New International Commentary on the New Testament. Grand Rapids: Eerdmans, 1996.

Morris, Thomas. *Our Idea of God: An Introduction to Philosophical Theology.* Vancouver: Regent College Publishing, 1997.

———. *The Logic of God Incarnate.* Ithaca: Cornell University Press, 1986.

O'Brien, P. T. *The Letter to the Hebrews.* Pillar New Testament Commentary. Grand Rapids: Eerdmans, 2010.

Owen, John. *The Works of John Owen.* Vol. 3. Edinburgh: Banner of Truth, 1966.

Rankin, William Duncan. "Carnal Union with Christ in the Theology of T. F. Torrance." PhD diss, University of Edinburgh, 1997.

Sabourin, L. *Sin, Redemption, and Sacrifice: A Biblical and Patristic Study.* AB 48. Rome: Biblical Institute, 1971.

Seng, Kang Phee [P. S. Kang]. "The Concept of the Vicarious Humanity of Christ in the Theology of Thomas Forsyth Torrance." PhD diss., University of Aberdeen, 1983.

Stamps, Lucas. "You Asked: Did Jesus Assume a Fallen Human Nature?" The Gospel Coalition Blog. Dec. 19, 2012. https://www.thegospelcoalition.org/article/you-asked-did-jesus-assume-a-fallen-human-nature.

Sumner, Darren O. "Fallenness and Anhypostasis: A Way Forward in the Debate over Christ's Humanity." *Scottish Journal of Theology* 67/2 (2014) 195–212.

Swinburne, Richard. *Responsibility and Atonement.* Oxford: Oxford University Press, 1989.

Tanner, Norman P., ed. *Decrees of the Ecumenical Councils.* Vol. 1. Washington, DC: Georgetown University Press, 1982.

Tomlin, Chris. "Jesus Messiah." *Hello Love.* Compact Disc. Sixsteps Records. 2008.

Torrance, Thomas F. "Atonement and the Oneness of the Church." *Scottish Journal of Theology* 7/3 (September 1954) 245–69.

———. *Atonement: The Person and Work of Christ.* Milton Keynes: Paternoster, 2009.

———. "The Atonement the Singularity of Christ and the Finality of the Cross: The Atonement and the Moral Order." In *Universalism and the Doctrine of Hell*, edited by Nigel M. de S. Cameron, 225–56. Grand Rapids: Baker, 1992.

———. "The Atoning Obedience of Christ." *Moravian Theological Seminary Bulletin* (Fall 1959) 65–81.

———. *Conflict and Agreement in the Church.* Vol. 2, *The Ministry and Sacraments of the Gospel.* London: Lutterworth, 1959.

———. "The Distinctive Character of the Reformed Tradition." In *Incarnational Ministry: The Presence of Christ in Church, Society, and Family: Essays in Honor of Ray S. Anderson*, edited by Christian D. Kettler and Todd H. Speidell, 2–15. Colorado Springs: Helmers and Howard, 1990.

———. *Divine Meaning: Studies in Patristic Hermeneutics.* Edinburgh: T. & T. Clark, 1995.

———. *The Doctrine of Jesus Christ: The Auburn Lectures 1938/39.* Eugene, OR: Wipf & Stock, 2001.

———. "The Doctrine of the Virgin Birth." *Scottish Bulletin of Evangelical Theology* 12 (1994) 8–25.

———. "The Evangelical Significance of the Homoousios: Sermon on John 5:17." *Abba Salama* 5 (1974) 165–68.

———. *God and Rationality.* Oxford: Oxford University Press, 2000.

———. "The Goodness and Dignity of Man in the Christian Tradition." *Modern Theology* 4/4 (July 1988) 309–22.

———. *The Ground and Grammar of Theology.* Richard Lectures. Charlottesville: University Press of Virginia, 1980.

———. "Incarnation and Atonement: Theosis and Henosis in the Light of Modern Scientific Rejection of Dualism." *Society of Ordained Scientists.* 7 (Spring 1992) 8–20.

———. *Incarnation: The Person and Life of Christ.* Milton Keynes: Paternoster, 2008.

———. *Karl Barth: Biblical and Evangelical Theologian.* Edinburgh: T. & T. Clark, 1990.

———. "Letter to the Editor." *The Monthly Record of the Free Church of Scotland* (March 1984).

———. *The Mediation of Christ.* Colorado Springs: Helmers and Howard, 1992.

———. "The Place of Christology in Biblical and Dogmatic Theology." In *Essays in Christology for Karl Barth,* edited by T. H. L. Parker, 13–37. London: Lutterworth, 1956.

———. *Preaching Christ Today: The Gospel and Scientific Thinking.* Grand Rapids: Eerdmans, 1994.

———. "Predestination in Christ." *The Evangelical Quarterly* 13/2 (1941) 108–41.

———. *Reality and Evangelical Theology.* Downers Grove: InterVarsity, 1982.

———. *The School of Faith: The Catechisms of the Reformed Church.* New York: Harper, 1959.

———. "The Soul and Person in Theological Perspective." In *Religion, Reason and the Self: Essays in Honour of H. D. Lewis,* edited by Tewart R. Sutherland and T. A. Roberts, 103–18. Cardiff: University of Wales Press, 1989.

———. *Space, Time, and Incarnation.* Edinburgh: T. & T. Clark, 2005.

———. *Space, Time, and Resurrection.* Edinburgh: T. & T. Clark, 2000.

———. *Theological Science.* Oxford: Oxford University Press, 1969.

———. *Theology in Reconciliation: Essays Towards Evangelical and Catholic Unity in East and West.* Eugene, OR: Wipf & Stock, 1996.

———. *Theology in Reconstruction.* Eugene, OR: Wipf & Stock, 1996.

———. *The Trinitarian Faith.* Edinburgh: T. & T. Clark, 1995.

Vanhoozer, Kevin. *The Pastor as Public Theologian: Reclaiming a Lost Vision.* Grand Rapids: Brazos, 2015.

Van Kuiken, Jerome. "The Relationship of the Fall to Christ's Humanity: Patristic Theology as an Arbiter of the Modern Debate." PhD diss., University of Manchester, 2013.

Wainwright, William. "Original Sin." In *Philosophy and the Christian Faith*, edited by Thomas Morris, 31–60. Notre Dame: University of Notre Dame Press, 1988.

Wright, N. T. "The Meaning of *Peri Hamartias* in Romans 8,3." In *Studia Biblica III: Papers on Paul and Other New Testament Authors*, edited by E. A. Livingstone, 453–59. JSNT Supplement Series 3. Sheffield: JSOT, 1980.

Scripture Index

Made in the USA
Monee, IL
06 December 2019